CREATIVE PLACE-BASED ENVIRONMENTAL EDUCATION

Children and Schools as Ecopreneurs for Change

Hawthorn Press

First published in Norway in 2015 by Fagbokforlaget Vigmostad & Bjorke AS under the title *Kunnskap for Ei Felles Framtid* © 2018 Jorunn Barane, Aksel Hugo and Morten Clemetsen, 2015.

Jorunn Barane, Aksel Hugo and Morten Clemetsen are hereby identified as the authors of this work in accordance with section 77 of the Copyright, Designs and Patent Act, 1988. They assert and give notice of their moral right under this Act.

Hawthorn Press

Published by Hawthorn Press, Hawthorn House,
1 Lansdown Lane, Stroud, Gloucestershire, GL5 1BJ, UK
Tel: (01453) 757040 Email: info@hawthornpress.com
Website: www.hawthornpress.com

Typesetting by Lucy Guenot
Translated by Nathan Large
Printed by Henry Ling, The Dorset Press, Dorchester

This translation has been published with the financial support of NORLA.

Printed on paper sourced from sustainable managed forests and elemental chlorine free.

British Library Cataloguing in Publication Data applied for.

ISBN 978-1-907359-73-6

CREATIVE PLACE-BASED ENVIRONMENTAL EDUCATION

Children and Schools as Ecopreneurs for Change

Jorunn Barane, Aksel Hugo, Morten Clemetsen

Hawthorn Press

CONTENTS

FOREWORD

Beacon of Hope

On a windswept peak above Sognefjorden a lone watchman scans the horizon on a frigid November night. Suddenly, from across the vast undulating landscape to the West, a bright orange flame erupts out of the darkness. Struggling against the wind, he takes a torch from the small fire that warms his hut, and ignites a pile of wood saturated with pine tar. The signal from the watchtower blazes out a warning to the local inhabitants of the villages and farms far below that danger is imminent.

Thousands of miles away, another watchman from a mesa top in the Central Highlands of Arizona lights a similar fire to warn his clan that an enemy had been sighted. His fire alerted another watchman on a distant butte silhouetted against a dark sky embroidered with stars.

Half a millennium later, I traveled from the mesas and canyons of the American Southwest to the fjords, mountains and forests of my Scandinavian ancestors; the oaks, maples, birch and pine forests felt very familiar to where I grew up in the northern Midwest. As a professor of Environmental Studies, I feel more at home when I can identify the trees and plants, understand the geology and watershed, and unravel the human history that brings relevance to the landscape, and helps me to be able to read and interpret the place where I happen to be. But to belong to a place is something far more challenging, and becomes a journey that requires being very attentive, with one's mind as well as one's heart.

What is Home? And what does it mean to belong?

When I first arrived in Norway, in 1991, I felt out of place. The landscape, while incredibly beautiful, was not familiar; the language sounded like English spoken backwards. I was a guest instructor, working for room and board at a place called Olavskulen Folkehøgskule, on the island of Bømlo. I could not pronounce the name of the place that would become my second home.

Øystein, whose name means island rock, was one of the first Norwegians I met. He could speak English! He became my best friend.

It has now been more than 25 years since I first lived and taught Friluftsliv (free air life) on the island of Bømlo. Several years later I was invited as a guest professor at Telemark University College in one of Norway's first interdisciplinary environmental studies programs, where I co-taught a course on Eco-philosophy that included perspectives of Arne Næss and Deep Ecology, a philosophy that promotes the idea that an ecological understanding is a critical foundation for sustainability.

I have had the opportunity to study and teach in several different bioregions, including Mexico's Gulf of California and the Sonoran Desert and Colorado Plateau Bioregions of the southwestern United States, and in cultural settings as varied as Seri, Navajo, Hopi,

Mexican and Norwegian communities of fishermen, farmers and ranchers. These experiences led me to wonder:

1. How does landscape influence culture?
2. How does culture, through mythology, folklore and traditions, influence contemporary cultural landscapes and how people view the place where they live?

I incorporated these questions in a class I have taught with students from Prescott College: 'Explorations of Norway Nature and Culture'. In this class, we study relationships between landscape and culture in a variety of places, including Sogn Agricultural College in Aurland, at the head of Sognefjorden, the longest fjord in the world.

I first met Jorunn Barane when she was visiting her brother, Øystein. I had heard that Jorunn spent summers as a young girl in the mountains with sheep, goats and cows and was able to call in cows by singing in the hauntingly beautiful traditional style. She is now a nature educator and storyteller at Sogn Agricultural College.

The day we met, we traveled by boat to a small windswept island covered with purple heather, we gathered driftwood and ate fish we caught along with blåskjell (bivalves) that we collected from rocks submerged in the cold waters of the Norwegian Sea. By then, Bømlo had become a second home for me, and I had also learned enough Norwegian to understand how language is related to place and reflects a reality that connects people to their home.

I met Morten Clemetsen with my students at his modern office in Aurland. Morten, professor at the Norwegian University of Life Sciences, specializes in Landscape Planning and also served as a consultant within the World Heritage Area in the Sognefjorden region. Morten is also involved in the restoration of Sinjarheim, a 600 hundred-year old mountain farm perched 300 meters above a cascading river that carved the Aurlandsdalen valley.

This past summer I was invited on a 'storying wander' or wandering five-day trek, by Jorunn and Morten, and met Aksel Hugo, the third author of this book, who is the Principal of the Sogn Agricultural College.

The trek that Jorunn, Morten and Aksel orchestrated, with the assistance of other accomplished storytellers, intertwined the folklore of the valley with our conversations about place-base education. I gained a personal insight of how stories can expand our understanding of place, where generations of people have lived before us, and imagine how they viewed their lives and their surroundings, adding to the depth and richness of our own connection to place.

The expertise, wisdom and scope of understanding that Jorunn, Morten and Aksel shared with our group underscores the depth and commitment that has occurred in creating what the authors refer to as the Aurland Model. It is an amazing actualization of what can occur when you have a team with a vision and the complementary skills and will to make it succeed. By writing this book, the authors hope to share ways that teachers, students, storytellers, entrepreneurs, farmers, children, refugees and people with special needs can come together through a carefully designed and meaningful curriculum based on gardening and local agriculture. This can greatly enhance what has been traditionally taught in our schools and separated into subjects that are too often disconnected and lack relevance.

The book is written with engaging stories, clear examples, interlaced with educational theory and practical suggestions and questions of what to consider when planning a program that may occur in drastically different settings and circumstances. Examples of other place-based programs are described that occur in National Parks in Great Britain, Ruskin Mill and in the Uluguru mountains in Tanania.

I believe this book can provide a common ground between educational standards coming from the top, to information, experience, wisdom and creativity that come from the local and regional environments.

I have visited Aurland and the Sogn Agricultural College many times with my students. I consider their effort/project to be one of the most exciting and comprehensive place-based programs that I have encountered. I can visualize the thematic gardens raised by the children, the farm where the older students milk the goats and learn how to care for the animals, the local school, community and landscape, which no doubt influences a biased perspective. One of my challenges in writing the foreword is how I can possibly capture in words the emotions I have experienced with the landscape and cultural connection that I have experienced by being there. I deeply understand what the authors are attempting to explain, and I personally enjoyed the dance between theory, curriculum and story. I believe the uniqueness of this book is the interface and intertwining of theory, practice and place that involves asking significant questions related to place-based sustainability, agriculture and education.

On the fourth day of our trek, we made it to the highest point of the trail, well above the treeline. I gazed out across the alpine landscape to a distant peak to the southeast that I had climbed years before. I was now familiar enough with the landscape to know the name of the mountain was Gaustatoppen. I wondered if there were remnants of a signal tower and how this book, along with the work being done by dedicated people in Norway and around the world, is like lighting a signal fire that can be seen across the landscape causing another fire to be lit by another watchman. But this time it is not a warning fire, but a Beacon of Hope.

Douglas Forell Hulmes
Professor of Environmental Studies, Prescott College, Prescott, Arizona

PREFACE

The World Commission on Environment and Development, chaired by former Norwegian Prime Minister Gro Harlem Brundtland, laid the groundwork for the convening of the 1992 Earth Summit in Rio de Janeiro, where participating countries committed to drawing up national strategies for sustainable development. Looking back, we see the foundation for strategies for environmental education, new educational theories, policies, national and local initiatives informing Education for Sustainable Development (ESD). We also see the formation of place-based strategies, as in Local Agenda 21, focusing on new theory, policies and national or local initiatives for sustainable community development. This book's unique perspective brings these two strategies together into an action research question: 'How can schools become agents of creative, place-based sustainable development?'

Inspired by Rio, this book is the result of 20 years' work with schools, NGOs, businesses and colleagues, all sharing relationships to the physical landscape of Aurland in Sognefjord, Norway. We hope the story it tells also conveys something universal to inspire others to find a distinctive learning model for their own setting. The Norwegian edition has, in the English translation process, been transformed into a 'second edition', with international readers in mind. We have added British and Tanzanian examples and removed some Norwegian references, revising the book to make it as accessible and transferable as possible. Our thinking has continued to ripen, particularly regarding the kind of creative educational leadership that is needed.

Sustainability cannot be achieved without a deep sense of community and connection with the earth and with life, the foundation being education that fosters empathy, equality and democratic transparency. Education should not be regarded only as preparation for shaping sustainable futures. As this book tries to show, sustainability lives inside learning processes that no longer disconnect us from nature's life processes and from social context.

It could be said that the aim of evolution is love, with creativity its driving force. So, what else is sustainable education, but a way to realise the Agenda 21 imperative of 'think globally, act locally'? For us, schools seeing themselves as ecopreneurs for change will help build common wealth for all. Hence, our approach links with Hawthorn Press's Social Ecology series for enabling a more free, equal, mutual and earth-caring society.

We thank everyone who joined our learning journey, in the Sognefjord region, in the Nærøyfjord World Heritage Area and in the teacher training programmes at the Norwegian University of Life Science, in particular Dr Erling Krogh in the Section for Learning and Teacher Education. We also thank the Ruskin Mill Trust for long-lasting cooperation, and Martin Large at Hawthorn Press for his great and persevering enthusiasm for this book.

Jorunn Barane, Aksel Hugo and Morten Clemetsen

Sogn Agricultural College (Aurland) and Norwegian University of Life Sciences (Aas)

INTRODUCTION

The Boat Is Broken

The fjord opens west towards the North Sea, glittering silver and green. The sky is blue. Far out, these colours meet and define the horizon. Nearer the coastline we can see small islands, skerries and bare rocks in the salt sea. And we know them all by name – this is the magic land of the faeries. In springtime, often in May, we row out to these islands. Our old rowing boat is newly painted and smells of tar. It has two pairs of oars and lies steady in the water.

Each spring we row out to the islands, jump ashore and run around. We can feel the heat coming from the rocks beneath our feet. The children look for purple thrift and seagull nests, hard to see because their eggs blend with the rocks. The gull's egg is large and grey with brown spots. We look for cracks and find a small beak picking a hole. We sit down to study the chick wanting to come out, dishevelled and small, with a yellow beak. In doing this we are studying life itself.

When we get hungry we make a driftwood fire and cook what we've found during the day in the salt sea water. It could be a crab, scallops or fish. We go beachcombing. Sometimes we find old shoes or soles and make up stories about them. Who were their owners and what were their fates? Was their ship lost with all hands? The story could be very dramatic. These islands are paradise and magical for us. They have everything we need. We don't go to church on Sundays; out here the spirit of creation surrounds us.

One cold winter's day we stand in our bright blue house by the fjord, looking out of the kitchen windows. The thin nylon curtains move in the draught. The storm whips the green waves in the bay and they have white summits. We see it now: the old rowing boat, that was laid up secure on the wharf, has blown into that sea. We can see it pitching on the waves like a whale. Our father comes in, and we hold our breath. 'No', he says, 'we can't save it.' The boat is broken, split in two. We have to let it go.

The disaster was complete; we had lost the safe old tar-black rowing boat that had been our connection to the magical green islands in the west. It is right here that Jorunn's childhood story ends and the story of this book has its beginning. 'I had a strong notion', she says, 'that in the future I had to create connections to the world around me by myself.'

How do we build the bridge back to interacting with the living world? How can we feel at ease and at home in the world today? How do we find and sustain this state jointly, in a group, as colleagues or as a school, in a community or in society at large? It means learning to make links and see connections, to articulate emerging themes and to shift power relations. It involves a nuanced use of language, drawing attention to unexpected possibilities as they arise, inviting collective reflection and refashioning the meaning of success as we come to recognize the form it is beginning to take.

We can only really stay in touch with what is happening when we live into the moves we find ourselves making. Parker Palmer (1990, pp. 15–16) suggests that the challenge is to integrate contemplation and action. He writes, 'As adults we must achieve a complex integration between inner and other reality that supports both personal integrity and the common good'.

Is this something we can do as educators too – train young people and children to take the lead at school and in kindergarten? To learn how to shape oneself and one's surroundings in a sustainable way. To learn to act mindfully. To seek out our personal questions and what we care for. To decide what we devote our attention to as we live in relationship with each other and the land. To learn to take leadership in helping to bring about a sustainable future, based on our own inner values, local resources and trends in society.

Widening circles

> I live my life in widening circles, that reach out across the world. I may not ever complete the last one, but I give myself to it. (Rainer Marie Rilke)

At all times people have wandered and exchanged ideas and stories, traded goods, learned new skills and developed both culture and economy. New techniques of weaving and other crafts have spread through regions and countries, merging with local traditions to produce a multitude of different styles. The same with music, language and other expressions of culture. These evolutionary processes can take place in smaller or larger circles, between neighbouring valleys or along farther trade routes throughout the world.

In our own time, it is important to bear in mind that hunger, war and the quest for safety and shelter have in all times forced people to migrate. Refugees today are searching for a place to settle. Whether we be refugees or locals, the questions are the same: How can we understand and share our culture, stories and tradition, our language and landscape? What actually is home?

The widening circle is a metaphor for a new vision of a school that embraces this role of shaping the future in place. The idea of home takes on a new meaning: as a space for envisioning what is not yet there and putting our visions to work; a space where children and young people, together with people of all ages, *build a bridge* into the future. And this bridge will become the home ground where people can meet regardless of background, age, creed or nationality.

The stories of widening circles we share in this book are based on experiences connected to a particular landscape in Aurland and the Indre Sogn region. Through the particular, the book pursues a general pedagogical and methodological objective. We hope that it will inspire readers to see their own local school, community and landscape with fresh eyes. What visions and goals may be revealed for your school, your landscape and your community? What sorts of resources, hidden stories and opportunities may, circle by circle, be unfolded in your place?

In Part I we present an example of how to establish new learning spaces outside the classroom, in the school's natural and cultural surroundings. Hence the circles of the Aurland model, in which the garden is the innermost *space for growth*, followed by the farm and the space for work, and then, as the pupils grow, our *cultural landscape and history* and, furthest out, *the fjord, the river, the mountains* and *the wider world*. Through the spaces that have been created, a distinct process of development can unfold, both inwardly in the pupil and outwardly in the activities. The result is a double cultivation process, where 'growing people' connects to 'growing place'.

To extend outwards, one also has go deep. So Parts I and II are inseparable: only when we can substantiate with examples what it means to anchor a national curriculum locally do we have the power and direction to know what we wish to gain from dialogue with the world around us. In this question of power and direction we find all the challenges of our times. These are challenges a forward-looking school should seek to tackle and transform. To achieve a double cultivation process, a double reversal needs to take place. The first reversal has to do with reversed curriculum design, in which the national curriculum framework is transformed to serve the widening circles. The method of reversed curriculum design as a tool for transforming national curricula into local curricula was developed in close collaboration with the teacher education department at the Norwegian University of Life Sciences (NMBU). As a practical tool for local curriculum designers, it empowers schools and teachers to shape a grounded student journey through time and space. In this method the national learning outcomes are not at all neglected. On the contrary, they are all covered, and also firmly grounded in personal experience and independent reflection.

The second reversal, which is inseparable from the first, is pedagogical. Regarding learning as a result of participation, it begins by asking for the right arena to cultivate the right activity. If, for instance, we want to cultivate compassion, what will the arena and student journey look like. In Part II we show how the pedagogical reversal can be performed systematically. The tool we use is enactment analysis, mapping the kinds of inner engagement that the arena, activity and encounter will call forth. This empowers the educator to make implicit outcomes explicit.

In Part III we turn from the question of growing people and pedagogy to the growing places and community. We look at the same widening circles one more time, but now from the perspective of the place in its region, history and future. What is the school's role in knowing, teaching and co-shaping the place, landscape and region it is located in? And how can the evolution of a place and region involve and integrate newcomers – children, youth or immigrants? The tool we use to understand and integrate the different layers of this process is a conceptual scheme developed by the Scottish biologist and town planner Patrick Geddes. We also present a mapping tool that schools can use to detect the resources in widening circles of their own neighbourhood. In this third part of the book the model of transformative learning cycles includes not only pupils and schools, but all citizens and actors that share the same landscape.

Spaces to evolve and transform

The most important ethical responsibility of schools and teachers is to create spaces for newcomers to evolve and transform. Through 'new beginnings' a person grows step by step into the world. This is as true for the little child and the youth as it is for the refugee. Year by year we expand our fields of interest and practice. And these new authentic learning arenas provide new opportunities to foster inclusion, integration, development and transformation, both for the school and for pupils, teachers, school leaders and parents.

If education is to mean something beyond mere teaching, which is classically a process of filling pupils up with knowledge while they are seated, it must be seen as a process of engagement in the world through curiosity and work, interest and participation, resistance and enjoyment. But, first, space must be made for such experiential learning to unfold.

An essential condition is to connect with people who already know the place and have a meaningful connection with these areas. We need people who can lead us into unfamiliar contexts to help reveal to us the place's hidden potential.

This is true for anyone wishing to work pedagogically and creatively. That is why the particular learning arenas depicted in this book are only parts of the answer. We cannot simply duplicate someone else's model; we must understand and build on the underlying thinking, and work creatively from the individuality of our place and community. We must go on a 'treasure hunt' in our own surroundings to find and make the learning spaces that make sense and to look at the unique interplay there between human, nature and culture.

In the story of our efforts in Aurland we illustrate how values, responsibility and sustainability for the future can be cultivated when learning is based in place. When children are surrounded by meaningful activities, we don't need to invent them. The picture of Guro and the lamb on page 34 gives us a glimpse of the wordless dialogue in the innermost circle between you and me. This exercise is driven by the interaction between animal and human; Guro is practising being at home in the world. The relational space can later be extended, gradually, but only when dialogue between the internal and external worlds is in place. People were better at this in the past, when interdependence was a matter of survival. Today we need to approach the question of belonging consciously. When organizing space and activity we must learn to be present and mindful.

PART I

LEARNING IN PLACE: THE STORY OF THE AURLAND MODEL

Photograph: Cecilie Bugge

CHAPTER ONE

PLACE AND LEARNING

> A basic human need is to grow up in a cultural tradition one can call one's own, so as to achieve an identity – without identity, no whole human beings and no human freedom. … Identity is also a prerequisite for society and for democracy, for these need individuals who can speak up, contributing with something uniquely theirs.
>
> (Kvaløy Setreng 2014, p. 28)

Education for sustainable development seeks to make abstract knowledge more practical, more relevant and closer to life. In doing so, it opens the way for kindergartens and schools to work with partners outside school. By engaging in life through place-based learning and entrepreneurship, you can get to know oneself well enough to *create* from within and from the resources and distinctiveness of the place where you live. Through activities such as school gardening, or learning on the farm, it is possible to develop the self-esteem of the people who live and work in the local community. In shaping our spaces, we create our own stories and inspire young people and others to feel a sense of belonging, both locally and in the wider world.

What is a place?

Everything takes place. When this text was being written, when it is read, it 'takes place'. Literally. All thoughts and actions exist in a reciprocal relationship with where they happen. Thought and action help to make a geographic location into a place for us. Our own activity can turn even the most unassuming spot into a place, as long as we are aware of this connection.

We come to know ourselves by interacting with the world about us and meeting 'the other'. Whenever this meeting 'takes place', the foundation is laid for both individual and social growth. Access to places and the ability to engage in active dialogue with place develop us as people and equip us to take part in community life.

The concepts 'place' and 'landscape' are closely related. Both have a physical and geographical dimension; they are tangible and contain objects that everyone can relate to. At the same time, they represent memories, meaning and mental qualities, things we bear within us and that have value for each of us according to our individual biographies.

In this book we will use the concepts 'place' and 'landscape' in much the same sense. It may be an area that is small or large, urban or rural. What matters is that place and landscape are spatial realities that are shared by many. It is people's activities and consciousness of their surroundings that make a place or a landscape (Ingold 2000). In cultural and social terms, we can therefore regard the landscape as a 'meeting ground' (Phillips 2005).

Free access to nature and landscape is an important condition for democratic social development. This much is acknowledged in the core principles of the European Landscape Convention: all landscape has value and meaning for somebody. Not just tourist destinations and well-kept cultural landscapes, but also places in decay and without obvious value (see box).

The European Landscape Convention came into force in 2004. As of 2016, 38 countries have implemented this convention. Its primary purpose is to create awareness about the universal human right of access to landscape for purposes of identity, belonging, and fulfilling one's potential. Article 5 states that each country must recognize in law that landscape is an essential element in people's surroundings, an expression of the diversity of their shared cultural and natural heritage, and a foundation of their identity.

The Convention defines the concept of landscape thus: '"Landscape" means an area, as perceived by people, whose character is the result of the action and interaction of natural and/or human factors' (European Landscape Convention, Article 1a).

States that have ratified the Landscape Convention undertake to improve knowledge of their landscapes and the values they represent, and to promote training and education with a view to protecting, managing, planning and developing places and landscapes to satisfy future demands.

Articles 6a–c also specifically mention states' obligation to increase social awareness about landscape, and to develop school and university courses addressing the values attached to landscape, and how these should inform management and planning.

So what is 'place', anyway, and how can we make clear to everyone what we are about? As we understand it, there are several terms that are meaningful in different contexts, as shown in Figure 1.1.

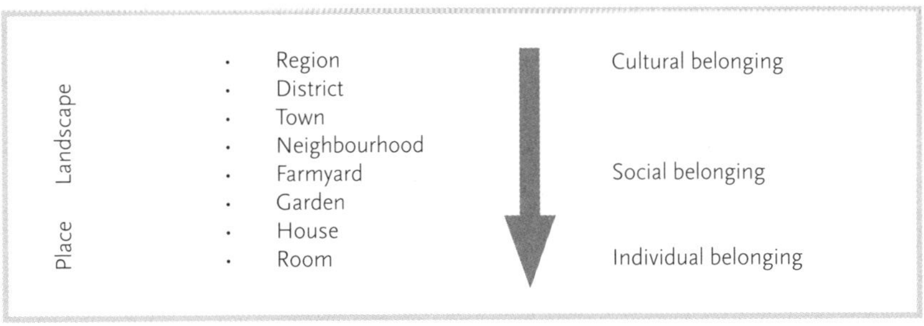

Figure 1.1 How we are bound to the world in different relational contexts.

The terms in Figure 1.1 lack the fixed boundaries of administrative and legal states, counties, municipalities or properties. Nevertheless, we can situate them on a scale, as shown. 'Landscape' is linked to the more overarching contexts, while 'place' is more local and closer to people's everyday lives and private spheres. The scale is therefore a sliding one between different forms of cultural, social and individual attachment to place.

So place and landscape are also a *common venue* where people's being can unfold in different ways. Cultural events, sports and festivals appeal to us in our region or district. Social gatherings and involvement in teams and clubs happen in towns or neighbourhoods. Interactions with our nearest and dearest take place in the home sphere

The landscape as a common venue

Much of the practical material in this book relates to landscapes and local communities in the west of Norway, especially in Aurland. Here, we shall briefly introduce these landscapes. Although the region is rather special, and despite its value as a tourist destination receiving more than 700,000 visitors every year, it shares many of the same qualities as other places as a venue for activities, experiences and new encounters.

Aurland is the only municipality in Sogn og Fjordane with a railway connection, and so we start at Myrdal Station, where the Bergen and Flåm lines meet, 867 metres above sea level.

It's chilly, with a hint of snow. It is early spring and snow still lies in big drifts on the valley sides, but the watercourses have opened up and huge quantities of meltwater are hurling down the steep mountain sides. The changeover from the morning Oslo-to-Bergen service goes quickly. Soon we are on the Flåm train looking down at the Navvy Road, which threads its way up the mountain and which, over 100 years ago, made possible the construction of the railway.

The Flåm Valley opens abruptly like a gigantic tear in the massif, part of a northern spur of the Hardangervidda. Here, softer phyllites among the basement rocks were no match for the mighty ice that tore off huge boulders and carried them out to sea – a distance of nearly 200 km. Gradually, as the ice melted and lost its power, more boulders, stones and gravel were left behind in the valley.

The water, having flushed out of deep channels, ravines and potholes, forms a tranquil river that in places flows through wide moraines on the valley floor. Along much of the Flåm Valley the river has allowed the growing of grass and wheat. As people migrated into the area they settled in hill farms, near the rich reindeer-hunting grounds, fishing lakes and grazing land in the mountains.

Later, they also began to use the cultivable and harvestable land on the valley floor and along the fjord. A comprehensive network of paths and trails linked fjord, valley and mountain and made it possible to plot the most incredible routes. Some of these old tracks are visible from the train as straight-cut lines through the pale dead grass from last year.

The community of Aurlandsvangen, as viewed from Prest, 1400 metres above sea level. Flåm can be glimpsed at the far end of the fjord. Photograph: Morten Clemetsen

It takes time to descend from the mountain. The train continues past old abandoned farms and, eventually, places that are still in active use. Soon we see sheep and gambolling lambs in the infields. We see old and newly cleared pastureland enclosed with netting. Flocks of young goats scamper about and nibble spring grass and fresh shoots. They are part of the measures taken to conserve the cultural landscape of the valley, to liven up the view from road and railway and, not least, to test new ways to generate wealth in the local economy.

The railway finally levels out; the last bit to the terminus in Flåm and the Aurlandsfjord passes through a well-tended cultural landscape along the salmon-bearing stretch of the river. The many fruit and berry orchards signal the importance of these crops for the area's farms and gardens.

At Flåm, there are a number of options for onward travel. Perhaps an early cruise ship has docked already – which can easily carry more than double the 1,700 residents of Aurland municipality. It can get crowded in Flåm on such days, and the centre is carefully designed to cope. Many passengers are picked up by buses that take them to other adventures along the E16, the trunk road between Oslo and Bergen.

If we hop on the year-round ferry to Gudvangen, we can see other districts in the area and the mountains that tower up to 1,800 m above sea level before rounding off into a cornice of perpetual snow.

First we pass by Aurlandsvangen, the municipal centre. Aurland Primary and Secondary School and Sogn Agricultural College lie either side of the valley road, a little way up from the fjord. Farms lie along the open and west-facing sides of the fjord. You can read about them in the Icelandic sagas.

Later the fjord turns to reveal the rural settlement of Undredal, nationally renowned for its goat cheese. Soon the ferry rounds a sharp ridge and enters the even narrower Nærøyfjord. We pass several hamlets before reaching Gudvangen, where the public bus waits to take travellers back to the Oslo–Bergen railway line.

The eco-school in Aurland

Innermost in the Aurlandsfjord is Sogn Agricultural College (SJH), an upper secondary vocational school specializing in ecological agriculture and horticulture. Since it has played a major role in the story of the Aurland paradigm, let's take a closer look at it. People have lived and worked in this place since ancient times. In the barrows on the site are traces of settlement dating back to early Celtic Christianity. The village vicarage has stood here since 1650. During the 19th century, the lay preacher Hans Nielsen Hauge (1771–1824) spread ideas of spiritual, social and economic freedom akin to those of the movement the Brazilian educator and social activist Paulo Freire initiated in South America a century-and-a-half later. Hauge (1961) was interested in farming and industry, always connecting spiritual renewal to the social and practical needs of ordinary people. The Haugean movement thus grew strong in agricultural areas like Indre Sogn.

SJH and the 'Ø-label', Norway's organic certification. Photograph: SJH

As farming became more market oriented, the first shoots of organized agricultural training appeared. Disruption of food imports during the First World War prompted the authorities to support measures to increase domestic production. The climate of Indre Sogn had already proven favourable for livestock and horticulture, and in 1917 the agricultural college in Aurland was founded. From the very first day, its doors were open to both sexes, which was doubtless a novelty at the time. The curricula for the different subjects were also groundbreaking. Jens Lunde, the school's founder, believed that if the new methods and ways of thinking proved successful, then many, if not all, farmers would need training in the future.

Responsiveness to change

Since then the school has been at the forefront of renewal and innovation. Might this be connected to the initial vision? How important is it to share a vision of the future, one that is inclusive and representative? Over the years, new pupils have brought new values and impulses to the school and community. From the outset, organic horticulture was an elective subject. If you wanted to weed and tend the organic garden, it had to be done during free time, not school time. But many of the staff listened to the pupils, as well as to their own inner voice, and this led to the entire school converting to organic production in 1989. Today it has the use of 25 hectares of arable land and 10 hectares of fertilized pasture. It also co-owns approximately 3,000 hectares of mountain pasture. SJH is the only agricultural college in the country whose entire holdings are certified organic.

The story of SJH mirrors those of Western Norway's small-scale farmers, whose survival has depended not just on resourcefulness and trust in fundamental values and knowledge, but on openness to the wider world and to changing needs and circumstances. The ability to adapt quickly is today more important than ever. The school has been threatened with closure for 30 years and its prospects have at times looked bleak. Yet it has remained true to the principles it was built on. At the same time, it has listened to the concerns of the young people who attend it – questions relating to the ecological and social crises in the world and springing from the reality they experience. Visions for a sustainable future must continuously be renewed. Socio-ecological transition does not proceed from a frozen ideal but unfolds in connection to the realities you face. This is a central element in transformative learning, to which we shall return in Parts 2 and 3.

Situated and sustainable learning

An overarching aim of ecological literacy is to bring about a fundamental change in our relationship with the world, so that we may interact considerately with humans and animals. This involves not just our conduct towards outer nature, but our relationship with inner nature as well. Whether you are planning to enrol at the agricultural college or are simply attending a short course, on your first day at SJH you can expect to be sent straight out to the fields to pick carrots, cabbage and leeks. Your first experience will be the smell of earth and the sense of fellowship. Practical exercises are performed in a group of like-minded people, with a focus on learning and on organic principles. It's much easier to get to know one another within the frame of manual work. The following day you may have to rise at dawn to milk the cows or mow grass with a two-wheeled tractor; the animals need feeding, after all. You find yourself mastering tools, mastering your body, stretching your limits a little more each day. You get to measure yourself against tasks that build new skills and knowledge within you and break new ground in the exteriority of the place.

The practical tasks demand concentration, confidence and calm. You have to be persistent, alert and, most of all, motivated. It is the weather, the season and the daily cycle that dictate what is to be done and when. The self-evident, necessary nature of the work, for example the fact the cows must be fed and milked each morning and evening, does many pupils the power of good. On the weekends you can expect to be sent into the mountains to milk goats. You will witness teachers and local farmers in dialogue with landscape and animals and see how they respect nature and take care of it. Even slaughter is carried out with respect and gratitude towards the animal; one must give and one must take. 'It's the meaning of life', said a local farmer, 'to see a seed grow into a plant or to help a suffering animal.' It gives you so much in return.

Little by little, you begin to see connections and understand that all things have their own time, rhythm, breath and fixed place through the year in interaction with everything else. You encounter something that is inherently true, that you can understand and stand for. Outer and inner values are aligned, the values of the place and the self converge, and you feel that you are on firm ground – a condition for developing identity and belonging.

> Education should view individuals as moral beings, accountable for their decisions and responsible for their actions; with the ability to seek what is true and to do what is right.
>
> (National Core Curriculum 1997, p. 9)

The meaning of land work is often tangible and obvious and closely connected to life processes. It involves cultivating attitudes, mastery and concrete purpose. With nature's help we can develop personal capabilities such as independence, responsibility, creativity, the ability to understand ourselves and our reactions, the ability to cooperate with others, and ethical awareness. These qualities are crucial to functioning in society today. They can be learnt in one context and be useful in others. Holistic skills are developed in concrete contexts. One learns by doing, but this is not enough: pupils must also be aware of what they are learning and why. Teachers also need to draw attention to what is happening to them on a personal level. We must attend to things that do not immediately lend themselves to measurement, like helpfulness, love of learning, and joy in wisdom and knowledge. We live in a highly fragmented world, and our ability to see connections is no longer a given. We are surrounded by a mass of information that does not explain anything, but rather rips up the connections between the world and each individual.

In the following chapter, we will demonstrate how to create spaces for learning by making use of the whole landscape and place. In Aurland, a number of learning arenas have been established and linked to learning objectives and activities in the curriculum.

CHAPTER TWO

DEVELOPING LOCAL CURRICULA

The Aurland model that we are going to introduce did not happen overnight. The emerging circles of the model, as outlined in development work, on flipcharts and in reports, are now familiar to us. The model became real because it was built and refined with pupils through place-based activities. The circles represent the ever-widening student journey of experience, activity and education. We had broken new ground and could communicate this vision both to colleagues and to the wider community of expertise. Our voices were heard and our model was noticed. Place-based learning became a planning priority at SJH. Step by step, a new community of peers and competence across vocational and academic arenas of education has been built.

Developing learning arenas locally is a long-term process. The work starts small but at the same time requires long-term direction and clear methods. In this chapter, we introduce principles and methods to help schools, teachers and resource managers to develop local learning arenas and curricula.

Looking back, we can identify four main steps in local place-based curriculum work:

1. Grounding: establishing the team and process.
2. Composing: shaping arenas and learning paths.
3. Anchoring: reversed curriculum planning.
4. Growing: renewing and extending the circles.

These are the steps of developing a local place-based curriculum. Every step needs to be firmly anchored and clearly formulated before participants can move on to the next one. Steps 3 and 4 will have to rotate each year, since new activities will constantly be introduced and existing ones modified. Local curriculum work acts as a 'translator' between the articulation of a locally formed learning path and its quality assurance with respect to academic learning objectives and the National Core Curriculum (NCC). By virtue of such an alternation between imaging and anchoring, the place-based curriculum is in a constant state of dynamic change and renewal in response to the changing identities and needs of pupils, school and place. One can start small with one or two year groups and then progressively convert the school, year by year, much as farmers do when they convert to organic practices. The timescale for completely converting to organic operations can be ten years. Schools must also allow more than a year for these processes to mature within the tension between old work patterns from the past and new ones for the future.

Grounding: establishing the team and process

The work needs to be firmly anchored among the school's leaders and educational environment. It helps to frame it as a project with (1) clearly defined goals and mandate, (2) a timescale and (3) the support of school management. A common approach is to form a project team that includes the headteacher in a key development role. Anchoring is not just an inward process; it is also important to gain support from appropriate partners outside the school. The model adopted in the example presented here was one of formal partnership agreements.

Once a project team has been established and a long-term undertaking has the support of the administrative and educational leaders of the school, the work of designing a local curriculum can get underway. Crucial in this phase are good teamwork, organization and routines for planning, implementation, follow-up work and passing on learning to the next cohort. In our case, the 'driver' role alternated among participants during the different phases of the process. It's crucial that partner (the place-based arena), teacher and school make a team that shares responsibility and agrees on goals, steps and content for practical activities and their corresponding learning. We were fortunate that alongside our pilot project we were also able to offer courses for teachers and farmers in place-based learning, which were structured as an action research project. This meant that all experience of the project could be shared, and that all contributions, successful or less successful, were equally important to the learning process. The curriculum design we explored can be customized and also anchored in a mode of working where learning can be passed from teacher to teacher and from year group to year group.

Composing: shaping arenas and learning paths

Systematic mapping of a place's resources is planning work. Step by step the pupils are led in ever-widening circles of activity into the place and the landscape.

Each activity along this journey will involve elements of outer and inner participation that can be examined in a situated learning analysis. Our decision to focus on grain in Class 1 (age six) and sheep in Class 3 (age eight) is the result of a double mapping, first of subject content and learning objectives, then of potential learning arenas that can be linked to in the school's vicinity. The plan is a creative product, a composition, whose score is the annual cycle. The activities must fit into periods, as notes do on a sheet of music, and within these periods the melody is the pupils' movements and participation in the landscape. In this work – just as in music – *themes* help to bind the composition together in wider movements.

Local place-based curriculum design must alternate between two poles: the whole and its parts. On the one hand, it is necessary to go into the detail of each activity, to know what one wants to achieve in terms of learning objectives, basic skills and educational goals. On the other hand, as a composer one needs to see the bigger picture: what kinds of learning arena, task and learning objective are appropriate for each year group? Such is the work of forming the plan and letting it evolve in a creative process, based on what pupils and place can give each other at the different stages of the youngsters' growing up. Each school must form their local curriculum around themes and activities that are locally and regionally relevant to them and that will stimulate pupils' interest in and enable them to interact with their surroundings. Each of the eight schools in The Living School project (1996–2000) wove a wholly distinctive curricular story (Hugo 2000). Sometimes the threads were spun within the school on the teachers' initiative; other times they came from outside: from the council, from local craft workshops, museums, nature management businesses, a fisherman, a hostelry undergoing renovation, old people's homes, municipal farms, market gardens, etc.

Each local curriculum process is a story in itself, and the story must be allowed to unfold, grow and become something of its own. Distinctiveness must find a place again in schools that have become more and more alike, where everyone marches in lockstep. Traditionally, each place had its own types of agriculture, suited to the local environment. In the future each place can have its wholly local school, whose pupils will be active place developers.

Anchoring: reversed curriculum planning

Educational goals and curriculum goals can be targeted through the selection of age- and subject-appropriate work tasks and learning tasks. To ensure that this work is long term and structured, academic curriculum goals should be linked to meaningful activities and arenas through the course of the seasons and from year group to year group. When this process is underway locally with the purpose of developing place-based local curricula, it may be called 'local place-based curriculum work'. It is 'reversed' because we *start* by developing meaningful activities and learning arenas in the annual cycle based on theme and year group.

The educational goals and academic goals can be joined up with the help of the choice of theme, learning arena and learning task. Only then do we map what skills, knowledge and competences the given activity and student journey will yield.

For a number of years, the teacher training programme at the Norwegian University of Life Sciences (NMBU) in Ås has been developing a tool known as 'reversed curriculum planning'.

In Figure 2.1 the arrows are two-directional because the process can start at a particular place, in a particular task or in an academic or pedagogical idea. How work tasks and learning tasks are composed must follow from one's chosen focus. Asking what kinds of participation are involved in a work task helps clarify what can be achieved academically and educationally through the activity in question. In Chapter 3 we give a series of examples of what skills and competences a particular activity can yield.

After the skill requirements of the work task have been analysed, a relevant learning objective is chosen in the tension between arena and curriculum. Then it's time to plan the learning activities. Sometimes a work task is so complex that pupils can only engage with parts of it in a learning situation; other times the task can be placed in a larger context in order for pupils to find it meaningful. The choice of work task may be determined by points in the curriculum, pupils' interests, local opportunities and financial constraints. Work tasks should relate to the needs of the community or take into consideration ecological contexts (Krogh 2010).

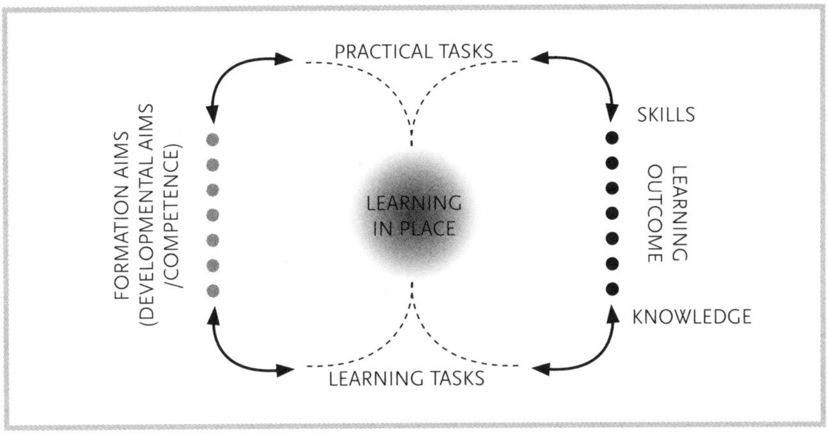

Figure 2.1 Reversed curriculum design. The figure shows how authentic learning arenas can integrate practical tasks and learning tasks – and how subject-specific learning outcomes and human developmental aims relating to transformative education can thereby be integrated.

As a basic rule, teachers and lesson planners should ask themselves: Which particular learning arena and learning task will give the pupil the resilience, experience, ability or understanding we are looking for? What is it important to experience at this age, in this class? As at Ruskin Mill (see box on pp. 126–33), the question can also be asked of special needs education: what learning arena constitutes the optimal learning environment for the special strengths or challenges of this particular pupil? To perform such an analysis successfully, the teacher has to *imagine* what the learning task actually does to the pupil. What skills does it require – cognitively, socially, etc.? Thinking like this gives new and richer meaning to the idea of special needs education.

Growing: renewing and extending the circles

The Aurland model evolved in stages, the number of year groups and arenas growing annually. Each circle takes time to develop, and also to trial and improve. It is vital to establish good practices for passing on learning, material and knowledge between teachers, so that classes can build on the work of their predecessors. Once again, it is a question of interaction, and of organizing the development of subjects with colleagues *over time.* The formulation of local curricula is a creative activity that generally starts modestly with a handful of classes and subjects, and then extends over the years to encompass all year groups. In our case we started in kindergarten, then worked up through the years with our pioneer class, routines and learning being consolidated in the groups following in their footsteps.

CHAPTER THREE

THE AURLAND MODEL

Aurland Primary and Secondary School (ABU) caters for children up to Class 10. In 2016 it had 145 pupils. Aurland municipality bought the plot in 1970 on the grounds of SJH, where a croft had once stood. The new school was built on the site in 1974. Aurdal, as the farm at the agricultural college used to be called, with its long history and rich natural resources, was the starting point for the development of the Aurland model.

The work germinated in the early 1990s with a school garden, at which stage many teachers were already busy with a number of community projects. It was followed up in connection with the Living School pilot project which ran from 1996 to 2000. It was later extended, both as part of the yearly curriculum planning process and in new pilot schemes of place-based entrepreneurship and learning at SJH, and regionally in Nærøyfjord World Heritage Park.

In light of their earlier efforts and local involvement, the two schools were invited to take part in the national Living School project, led by the Norwegian College of Agriculture.[1] During the four years of this experiment we had the chance, through courses and mentoring, to develop our projects and start new ones (Hugo 2000). Through networking, practical exercises and reflection, parents, teachers, and local organizations and businesses had the opportunity to open their eyes to, and articulate, their own setting and its possibilities. The positive response of experts and new colleagues told us we were on the right track and that our values and those of our place could contribute to learning for a sustainable future. So ABU teamed up with the farm at SJH to develop a local curriculum, starting with its own garden and continuing with the use of the college farm as a learning arena for Classes 1–10 (Parow 2000).

We were now one of eight pilot schools in Norway engaged with developing outdoor areas as learning arenas and farms as a pedagogical resource. The intention of Living School was for schools to produce, through local curriculum planning, a binding place-based curriculum by which, year by year, pupils would grow into the activities and culture of their community. Each school was to develop local place-based curricula across subjects and year groups, based on its particular identity and the resources of its environment. The idea was to bring school and pupils into contact with the nature, landscape, culture and community in their home setting.

After the project period ended, things quietened down, at least on the surface. Inwardly, there was a process of maturing and anchoring the importance of experience, activity, place and belonging.It is a process to be nurtured over the long term. One must persistently create new relationships and learning spaces, get others on board and make sure they are looking in the same direction. This requires careful allocation of resources and conscious reflection, exploring and working with shared values and visions for the future. The ABU website says, 'Living School focused originally on the school grounds and collaboration with the agricultural college. It has grown to embrace the whole municipality. Its main objective is that pupils shall develop a sense of local identity and contribute to the sustainable development of the municipality.'[2]

A curriculum needs to live and breathe. We must constantly push and create anew to move it forward. Every six months the farm managers meet with teachers to evaluate and update their work together. Many dynamic local people have joined in practical schemes and volunteer work associated with the project, and in 2009 we applied for funding from the county council to offer a new course on 'The Farm as a Pedagogical Resource', together with NMBU and the Resource Centre at SJH. There was a need to gather ourselves for a new push, to build new networks and meeting places, and to seek new learning. So three new accredited sessions were run, focusing on developing new learning tasks from a place's resources. At the Resource Centre many different courses are run that link to organic farming, training and the processing of local food. There is a Green Care programme in partnership with social services, which offers adapted work and training for pupils with special needs and for adults in work training. Guidance and competence-building are offered on how to use school farms as learning arenas. School classes from outside the region visit to get hands-on farming experience.

The principle behind the model is simple: in the course of each year, groups from kindergarten to Class 10 undertake different learning activities that are linked to a number of learning spaces or arenas out in the landscape and in place. Connecting activity and place poses a number of pedagogical challenges. In Aurland's case, years of trial and error have given us a stable foundation to build upon. Our seven main types of learning arena are: *garden, farm, cultural landscape, river, fjord, mountain, and the wider world,* as in Figure 3.1.

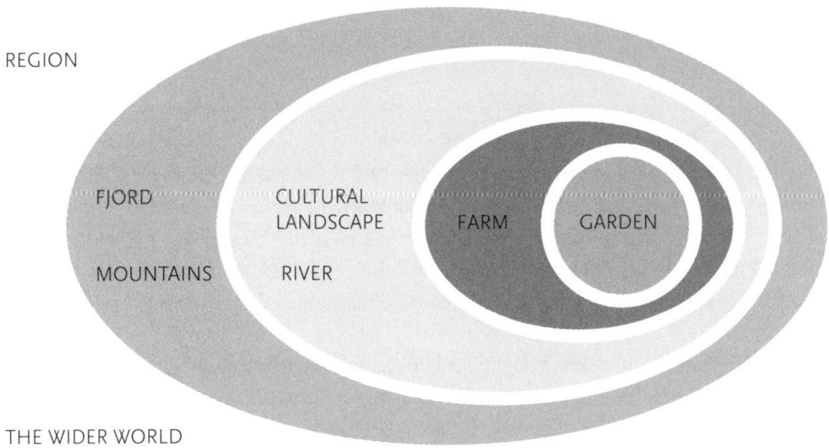

Figure 3.1. The widening circles of learning arenas we formulated in the Aurland model, from the local to the global. The model can be applied and adjusted to any landscape and locality.

The first step is to identify learning tasks for each school year which are embedded in the curriculum at hand (in our case so-called 'Knowledge Promotion' and the NCC). Each of these tasks must then be linked to a physical arena or learning space (Figure 3.1). Over the years, a range of projects has been implemented in the different learning spaces. Some take root in school plans and are carried out each year. Others have shorter lifespans: one or two years, depending what time, resources and focus we have at a given point. Good plans are dynamic. One must always be open to change and new ideas, and create afresh within existing constraints.

The development of the local curriculum in Aurland is based on many years of experience connecting three fundamentals: learning spaces, learning tasks and pedagogical tools (see Figure 3.2).Our concrete teaching plans arise from the interplay; arrows are two-directional because the starting point can be at a particular place (for example the garden), in a particular task (clearing trees and scrub from a barrow) or in a pedagogical idea (subject, curricular goal, overarching pedagogical aim). In Part III we shall return to this model and the question of how to use it as a method of working with local curricula.

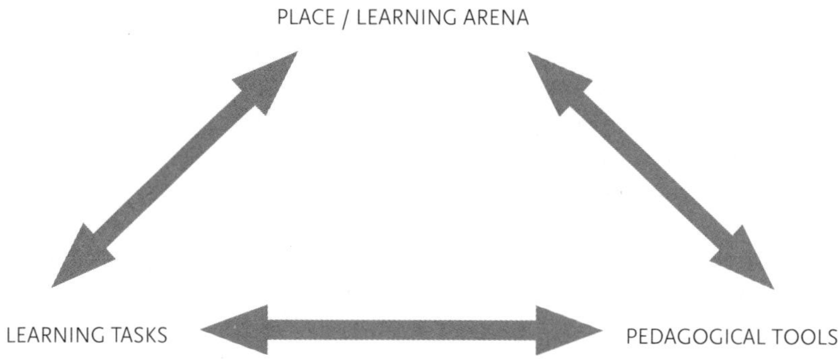

Figure 3.2. Meaningful activities connected to place yield both outer value and inner growth in the pupil.

Making space and breaking new ground

The first thing to do is to create new and safe learning arenas. This can be done together with pupils, parents and local experts. Many teachers are understandably wary of the chaos that may loom beyond the four secure walls of the classroom. We must make a clearing in the woods, a coherent space, where the youngest children, the pupils, teachers and parents can all feel at home. As Norberg-Schulz writes:

> Things intertwine, forest and thicket can stand for where we find ourselves. The path of discovery and searching is our path; it leads ever onwards, we forget where we come from and where we are going. We must make an opening in the 'thicket'. We must make a space, a clearing in the confusion. To make it a home, the space must be demarcated. (Norberg-Schulz 1993, p.1)

There are any number of ways to go about this. We may embark on an expedition and marvel at what we find, follow the brook and see where it goes. Even if it's only a space under a hazel bush or behind a barrow, the youngest ones will want to take their parents there next time and show them the hut they have built or the farm they have made from pine cones. We start close to the school buildings with the smallest children and venture further away as they grow. The yard and garden can be a hive of activity; here the children can study people working, plants growing and animals grazing.

The garden: space for growth and care

The learning arena

On the traditional Norwegian farm the 'tun' (related to the '-ton' of English place names) is the central yard around which the buildings are arranged. This space was the heart of the farm and the community in the old agrarian society. It was here that people spent much of their time, resources were processed and important events and festivals were marked through the seasons. The tun signalled the right to use the land on which their livelihoods depended. For this reason the placing of a farm's tun in the landscape was not left to chance. Tuns often occupy a prominent location, attuned to their surroundings and positioned to minimize the effort and energy needed to transport crops and manure between fields and tun (Ljøsne 1993).

Even though society has changed radically, the tun remains the fulcrum of an extensive cultural landscape that can offer clues about how the interplay between nature and humans has evolved over the ages. In many places, with house building and the shift from agriculture to urban development, the tun will be the last vestige of a vanished history.

The tun brings together several buildings, each with its own function but arranged to form a whole. Such a configuration can work well as a learning space, with its exciting inventory of animals, vegetable gardens, tools and equipment. Making it safe for pupils to learn here calls for good planning and cooperation with farm staff.

The garden is often part of the tun or can offer an alternative learning arena. Some schools have adopted the tradition of a school garden. A garden was originally a fenced-in area meant for a particular purpose like growing vegetables and flowers, or preventing calves or pigs from running loose. English 'garden' comes from the Old Norse word *gard* – meaning 'fenced plot'.

Spiren farm kindergarten

Right at the centre of the farm tun, in the old vicarage, you will find Spiren [Sprout] farm kindergarten. Here from an early age children forge connections and relationships by experiencing adults at work, for example as they pass by with tools, animals or produce. The kindergarten has a kitchen garden where each child has their own bed to plant with flowers and vegetables. Alongside the adults they can fetch milk, make apple juice and pick berries, vegetables and other produce needed for cooking in the kindergarten kitchen. The kindergarten also has its own chicken coop, ducks and rabbits.

Guro and the lamb. Photograph: SJH

Rabbit at Spiren. Photograph: SJH

Harvest at Spiren. Photograph: SJH

Every week the children visit the barn to be with the cows, goats and sheep. It is particularly fun in spring when the lambs and kids arrive; they are so nice to have on your lap. Following the seasons and entering into nature and the life of the farm – this is the pedagogical pillar of Spiren. Through the year, the children celebrate the seasonal festivals – Harvest, Michaelmas, Martinmas, the Advent Spiral, Sun Festival, Easter Garden and Summer Festival. In November, at Martinmas, you can watch a long line of figures singing, each holding a lantern they have made. They gather around the bonfire at dusk and listen to the story of St Martin. The evening has become a focal point for people in the district, when they light candles at the darkest time of the year.

In Norway's strategy for education for sustainable development (Kunnskapsdepartementet [KD] 2012, p. 11), we read that in early years education 'Taking care of nature and each other embraces both empathy and ecological responsibility, and shall be a natural part of children's learning process'. Children should have the chance to develop a love for nature and an understanding of the interaction between humans and nature. Further, 'It is important to promote the responsibility of natural and cultural stewardship, and for human life and health in the kindergarten. Understanding of sustainable development shall benefit daily life. Respect for life is fundamental' (KD 2012, p. 11).

Enactment analysis

When children have contact with animals, as at Spiren kindergarten, the wordless interactions of infancy are allowed to continue. The innermost circle between 'I' and 'you' is present again with the lamb who can be held on one's lap. The farm kindergarten has no need to devise new activities; they already fill the setting. The hens need feeding and give us eggs. The eggs must be prepared and served. In being part of such concrete sensory and living connections, one can feel at home. This is the second circle out from 'I' and 'you' – that of feeling at home among people, animals and nature.

These inner circles are about creating a sense of belonging, a home. The feeling always goes in two directions: I belong in the world and the world belongs in me. When they have this fundamental sense of assurance and attachment, children will be able to expand their relation to space, step by step, and venture into the unknown. This process will unfold, again, as a dialogue between inner and outer worlds.

Recent neurological research has shown how the dialogue in such relationship-building creates new pathways between the emotional brain (amygdala), the sensory and memory brain (hippocampus) and the reasoning brain (prefrontal cortex) (Albæk 2013). When one feels a sense of inner security and of being in a safe space, having learnt to master something or feel safe in life, then, yes, this is the right moment to reach out into new activities and experiences.

The school garden

The learning arena

The year was 1994 and the six-year-olds' time in kindergarten was at an end. Their newly built and freshly painted red schoolhouse awaited them. Everything was new: smart curtains, a new kitchen and fine new toys. The school lacked nothing – except scope and content. The new curriculum was not yet ready, so what was its first class to do? It took time for the partners to reach agreement. This allowed us teachers considerable latitude to take the pupils themselves as a starting point.

We had some wonderful, creative years with these eager, wide-eyed children and their toothless grins. We did what we had to do – we filled their days with meaningful work, practical activities, learning and celebrations, drawing on the different seasons and the resources available to us. There is perhaps no other age group that is more enthusiastic, inquisitive, open and eager to learn.

Just across the road from us is our closest neighbour, the agricultural college, on whose farm all of Norway's common livestock species are represented. It practises a tradition of mixed farming and has expertise in fruit and berries, vegetables, potatoes and grain. Wishing to make use of this, we liaised with farm staff and started to plot educational programmes. The first steps were modest, but it was just the beginning.

When spring came we wanted a garden of our own as well. The agricultural college lent us land (rent-free for as long as we cultivated it, and we continue to work it to this day). The caretaker helped to put up a fence to get us started.

Six-year-olds crave physical activity. The sight of adults active and at work performing visible tasks inspires them in their own games. The children fetched their bikes and attached trailers to them to make mini-tractors that we could load with small piles of stones. We measured out growing beds and sowed seeds in them: sunflowers, pea flowers, sugar peas and pumpkins. These seeds are large and easy for six-year-olds to work with. It is fascinating to examine the different kinds, some of which you can even eat. In the autumn our garden was filled with brightly coloured flowers which we could take inside and decorate the classroom with. Small children value highly anything that speaks to the senses. For six-year-olds, garden work is still a game in which they imitate adults. They run back and forth, work intensively for a moment, find a patch of ground and small creatures to study, and then in the next second they are off doing something else. As yet they lack the physical size and strength to work with heavy tools and earth. The garden has been an important focal point for parents and pupils over the years, with everyone helping out in the spring and a harvest feast of garden produce at summer's end. We also celebrate other festivals using the school farm as our base. During the first year, the whole neighbourhood took part in our Michaelmas Dragon Play.

Planting lettuce in the school garden. Photograph: Jorunn Barane

The class gathering blackcurrants. Photograph: ABU

Because the pumpkins grew so well the first season and the sugar peas were sweet, other pupils wanted to join in. 'We want a garden, too,' they said. And so the garden was extended, little by little, year by year, but never more than we were able to tend.

Enactment analysis

What do children learn from making and cultivating a garden? Were you to ask school-farm teachers from the 20th century, they would probably begin with the most obvious answer: children learn how to grow food. But to understand the value of gardening for schools, we must be aware of two other features of gardens which distinguish them as learning arenas. The first involves the *transformation of space*. To set up a garden is to refine a space: to step in, transform and make possible something that is beautiful and, at the same time, productive. Engaging with and creating things around us, we experience concretely that we can refine our surroundings. This involves understanding the conditions for growth and nurturing the space of that which will grow there. We tend, water, weed and toil to create the conditions for something to unfold. We are cultivating, certainly. We are learning a dialogue without words, tied to the interaction between *what is needed and what must be done*. This is what Aron Antonovsky (1987) describes as 'manageability'. So the first unique feature the garden offers as a learning arena is that we learn to refine our own surroundings.

The second characteristic is temporal. There's hardly another learning arena as slow as a garden! This point, the fact that it is not ready 'in no time', teaches us some-

Harvest dinner in Class 6, with produce from the garden, farm and the mountains.
Photograph: Jorunn Barane

thing. Through the example of the adults, the children learn to feel the 'long will' that follows what happens over the course of growth and development. *A will that cares all the way,* from start (seed) to finish (harvest). This is what marks out a good gardener. Not least in our day and age, the slow and persistent attention we learn in the garden is precious. The garden teaches us nurture and care in the most concrete form. It teaches us about ecology, too, and offers hands-on contact with nature. We learn to get our hands dirty and see and appreciate what is growing and what is beautiful. The fact that we can prepare our own food and share it at a banquet is, naturally, the icing on the cake. The social power of a meal that children have both grown and cooked together is tremendous. We realize that the garden is inexhaustibly rich in what it offers. What's more, the sight of adults taking spades in hand and doing meaningful work of this kind is something that matters in a society where children seldom get to see how work can lead to something growing.

The farm: place for work and processing

The learning arena

Infields encircle the tun, linked to it via a network of tractor tracks and paths. On farms with diversified production and crop rotation the land will be accessible along tracks and via crossings between fields, even at the height of the growing season. Open streams, buffer strips, clearance cairns, pastures and parcels of woodland give variety to the landscape and can be used in diverse learning situations. In many places we also find cultural monuments that tell of the farm's history. These include old buildings, stone walls, burial mounds, pollarded trees, avenues and dams.

When children start at ABU, across the road from the the agricultural college, they return to the farm for topic work, continuing until Class 10. In Class 1 they start with something close to home and essential: *grain*. In the field by the school they can sow, reap using small sickles, grind flour with the hand mill, bake bread and make porridge over an open fire.

The following year the pupils work with *potatoes* from planting to harvest and make products rooted in local traditions. Farm animals take them further out into the landscape: the *sheep* in Class 3, the *horse* in Class 4 and the *goat* in Class 5. This means trips to the pasture grounds, work with the cultural landscape, nights spent up in summer farms, and cheese-making.

In Class 3 the pupils learn about sheep by following them through the year. They come up to the barn in autumn and each child gets to choose a sheep, attach a bell to it and give it a name. Their next visit is at shearing time. They help to sort the wool into different categories, and take the best of it down to the school to card, spin or felt into items to use themselves or give away. Some years they use birch leaves or St John's wort to dye the wool or yarn a vivid yellow. This can be put aside and used for Easter decorations. Later in the autumn it is time for weighing and tupping. Come the spring it is exciting to see how many lambs are born.

Thus the children follow the sheep through the seasons and are there to watch when they are turned out to spring pasture.

Class 1 gathering grain. Photograph: SJH

David and Johannes. Photograph: SJH

Class 3's ewe has lambed. Photograph: SJH

In Class 6 the emphasis is on food and health, food preservation and milk processing. In the farm dairy the children make yoghurt, butter and cheese. They harvest vegetables on the farm, and also berries and fruit which they press and pasteurize into juice. They visit summer goat farms in the nearby mountains to join in the cheese-making and milking, and they pick wild berries for juice and preserves. In Class 7 they move further into the outfields and have outdoor classes, chopping wood, tending the cultural landscape by clearing footpaths and cultural monuments, or doing other work that is made light by many hands. Autumn brings fishing trips with the mountain ranger. Both Classes 6 and 7 work with composting in connection to the school garden and the question of managing waste so that it becomes a resource. After gathering in the harvest in September they hold a harvest thanksgiving festival in the longhouse, whose menu can include fish the children have caught themselves – grilled trout from the mountains – and bread and rolls made from the farm's own grain; and from the school garden herb butter, blackcurrant juice, potatoes and, last but not least, flowers to decorate the table.

One of the first things we did in the farm and fields was look for a safe, pleasant spot. We chose the apple orchard, which gets sunshine early in the spring and has big stones to climb on. The children invited their parents to help build leaf-huts in an old grove sheltered beside a stone wall. Thus we had made ourselves a new space. We had built ourselves a home a little further out but yet safe. So the activities could begin: yarn dyeing, fruit gathering, acting out and learning about the area's animals, insect study, making bird food over the fire, and summer parties with parents making bows and arrows.

Potato harvest in Class 2. Photograph: SJH

Harvest dinner. Photograph: SJH

The pupils liked the predictability of returning to the same area through the seasons, and together we could observe how the area was touched by our activity. The orchard changed by our spending time there doing place-based activities. In this way we cared for the area, developed it and made it a *place to be* – for other classes and kindergartens as well.

Enactment analysis

The farm is a highly diverse learning arena. Different tasks and activities can be combined and sequenced. The grain, potatoes and sheep are each part of bigger and meaningful working connections. The grain is sowed and harvested, ground into flour, baked and made into bread. Potatoes have to be planted, which requires chitting or pre-sprouting them beforehand; it's not till autumn, after the long summer holiday, that they can be dug up. Food's journey towards the table is also a natural component of this learning arena. Conversely, everything on our table can be traced back to the processes and conditions from which it has grown.

Put another way, the farm's operations lead us into the flow of time and the alternating seasons. With food and farming comes cultural history, linking to place and history both locally and globally. As they progress through school, the pupils gain a clear and tangible grounding in practical ecological thinking. Soil and soil formation, and compost and fertilization, introduce how death and life, and decay and growth, go hand in hand. In short, the farm functions as a great big practical ecology teacher. It offers a unique variety of tasks and gives pupils direct insight into big and concrete connections. Tillage, soil work, fodder production and tending livestock add up to a kind of organism in which parts and whole cohere. On top of this, there are machines and heavier tasks that require

Washing apples. Photograph: SJH

Apple pulp. Photograph: SJH

Pressing apple juice in Class 6. Photograph: SJH

strength and technical understanding. The farm is therefore a unique setting in which to differentiate tasks and adapt them to pupils' individual learning requirements.

Entrepreneurs in local produce

Apple pressing in the autumn is popular among all classes. Both Class 3 and Class 6 help with it each year. In Aurland there are many gardens with apple trees whose fruit is never harvested. Not everyone has time to make juice and preserves, so there is often much windfall fruit lying around that people are glad to give away. Pupils arrange to come with wheelbarrows and sacks to collect the apples. When they have a full load, they trundle up to the agricultural college where the old press is located.

The apples are washed, then mashed into a pulp and pressed through a cloth. Pressure is applied with a simple hand jack, and pure sweet juice starts to run into the bucket, without additives of any kind. It works every time. Next, the juice is heated up to 80ºC, pasteurized and decanted into plastic containers fitted with dispensing taps. Some classes have taken over 100 litres of juice back to school with them. It is served at parents' evenings, or sold in the village market to raise funds for class trips or other purposes. In this way the pupils help transform waste into a resource; windfall fruit are made into a nutritious juice that is both delicious and a source of income.

The cultural landscape: space for stories and history

The learning arena

Strictly speaking, 'cultural landscape' can mean all landscape that is influenced and shaped by people. Here we use the term to describe the areas that lie beyond the infields of the farm. Outfields may be fertile and offer good pasture but they often have thin soil, which makes them unfit for cultivation. They extend up the valley sides and ridges, places that tend to have good views. For centuries this landscape has been a mosaic of pastureland, hay meadows and pockets of woodland providing firewood and timber. In such areas the meeting of the natural resource base and human impact has led to great biodiversity.

All across this landscape are well-marked pack trails and footpaths. It is an important recreational space for the local community. The place is imbued with story, myths and legends. Where the 'hidden folk' lived you were supposed to tread lightly and avoid disturbing them.[3]

Landscape management

In middle school, the pupils help to clear footpaths and learn how to use axe and saw in cooperation with the rangers managing Nærøyfjord World Heritage Park. Class 5 is responsible for the culture trail to Turlifossen waterfall. The trees to be felled are picked out. The ranger talks about the different species, explaining what should stay standing, how the rest should be felled, why it is that we lay them in piles, and how these make the winter homes of insects, fungi and microorganisms. The pupils return to the same area several times in the course of the year and see how the landscape changes as they tend it. In this way they make the area their own.

Clearing a barrow

In early summer, Class 9 pupils from Bergen visit for hands-on farming experience. One of the topics they study is the conservation of cultural landscape. The Vikings who once lived on the site of the school farm left burial mounds dotting the landscape. Most of these barrows have been excavated and many of the finds are on display at the Historical Museum in Bergen. Our aim today is to impart knowledge about our cultural monuments through practical and active work. The barrows are nearly overgrown. Hazel and alder thickets have all but concealed them. Barrows are protected monuments and part of our cultural heritage, so we have a duty to keep them clear for public access and visibility from the road.

The pupils are equipped with billhooks, saws, axes and cutters. 'Can we make bows and arrows?', a 15-year-old cries, childhood memories coming back to him. Three classmates form a line at the base of the mound and move upwards as they cut. The air is filled with the sound of axes and concerted work. Hazel, ash and grey-alder stems fall to the ground. The teenagers cooperate, confer, inspect the results and drag the branches into a pile. They can master this. The work unfolds by itself; they know what needs to be done. The task allows them to be active and social without constant interruption. They find their own rhythm and can take off their thinking caps for a while. In this way they develop relationships with the place, themselves and each other.

The work is a good match for the age group. When the 19 pupils, divided into three groups, have finished, the barrow is visible again. During the break, we speculate who might have been buried here and how. Were they laid in a ship? Did they take tools and weapons with them to the otherworld? In the classroom that evening, there is time to reflect and to write in logbooks. What have we done today? Why and how? What are the names of the tools we used? What is the point of care and maintenance? This week the pupils have also made leaf mould, piled hay up to dry, made white cheese, thinned out plum and apple trees in the orchard and planted out herbs and vegetables in the fields.

In autumn, the same group returns for a week to help gather in the carrots, onions, pumpkins and potatoes. They help with the baking and press apple juice. They return to Bergen, taking with them top-quality produce, samples of which they can show off and serve at parents' evenings. When pupils are a little older, packhorses and tales of the valley lead them further into the landscape, where resources are harvested in sustainable ways.

Clearing the barrow. Photograph: Jorunn Barane

Preparing to burn leaves and cuttings, Class 9. Photograph: Jorunn Barane

Enactment analysis

The classroom that is normally these pupils' learning space is swapped for an authentic learning arena. 'Authentic' here refers to three conditions. First, the pupils meet a real barrow, not a textual, visual or digital representation of one. Second, their task is not designed to be approached abstractly; it is a real task. Third, the tools the pupils come into contact with are not abstract either; they are solid tools such as axe, sickle and saw. All three dimensions prompt a shift in teaching roles. The main role normally played by the teacher, that of spurring the pupils' motivation to get started, is transferred to the encounter between the pupil and a real task.

Internal and external motivation

The pupils are introduced to a task that has its own rationale, *a real need in the world,* in this case to clear a historic monument. When the teacher presents the task, it is given an external motive. Since the object is real, the pupils can now convert this motive into an internal one – one that they themselves can see the sense in acting upon. The reason for the task is thus linked to a real context of meaning. Indeed, even the material and tools may function as a motivator. When physical tools lie within reach, the will is galvanized to try them out. A tingling interest is aroused, the wish to touch them, hold them, try them out. Energies seeking an outlet stir only if they are set in motion. So one thing leads to another and the eagerness to work presses ahead under its own steam. Just as rhythms can spontaneously get the feet tapping, so the sight and smell of tangible tools and tasks can spark the motivation of some young people.

Authentic learning arenas are characterized by the way that motivation is generated in them. The task itself becomes the driving force, both of thought and of will. An important consequence is that the teacher–pupil relationship changes when motivation moves from being 'the teacher's job' to arising from real needs in real-life contexts. Teacher and pupil now have a less asymmetrical relationship: no longer does the one have the task of giving the other things to do. Once the work is underway, they are together in a shared task. Their mental and physical motivation leads into the third motivation field, sociality, which has to do with the experience of working together, with affinity and teamwork. Good interaction produces joy and meaning, both during work and, not least, in the breaks.

Self-motivation and self-regulation

Participation in simple and monotonous work hides many secrets. If we picture the barrow-clearing session in our mind's eye as if filming it from above, what do we see? Compared with what we might find if we filmed a lesson in a classroom, we see movement. But even before the outward movement there comes an inner one, *a motivation* to get started: internally, one way or another, the pupils must have committed to the task and made it their own. Whether they experience the task as a positive invitation or as an imposed burden depends on the context and atmosphere and on the adults involved. What has happened in the pupils' inward encounter with the task is therefore decisive for what we now see unfolding outwardly. We know that the origin of the motives that drive us, whether they come from outside or from within, makes a tremendous difference in our working life. In sustainable education the first question should therefore be: Where does motivation come from in the school's daily life? Is it generated from within through engagement with the world? The implication is that an act that is a part of a sustainable education process is different from one whose motive is driven by the school system. The difference lies not merely in the outward action, but also in how inner motive and outer action interrelate.

Keeping the bird's-eye view, filming from above, we see some tentative individual movements. Slowly but surely they gain in strength. They become more assured and find their own form and rhythm. Each pupil enters into the work in their own way. They gain skill, little by little, through using the tools. Though simple repetition and trial and error, each pupil lays the foundations for their own development. Flow and skill develop in each individual and in their working together as well. How to function as a team? Where to begin? When do we gather up the branches and where should we pile them? Who carries and who cuts? Each team finds its own ways to work together, even though this is the first time they have done anything like this. Out of the experience of a team's particular circumstances an interaction develops that is both practical and social. In other words, in educational terms, beneath the surface of monotonous clearing work there is a lot going on. The secret is that both head and hand can participate in self-regulated learning precisely when the task is so simple. And then, when one takes the lead, when the motive and content of the act have their own momentum, the human being *unfolds*. And when flow and the mood to work grow, limitations and inhibitions can be overcome: 'Can we make bows and arrows?'

Participation and empathy

Now we can flip perspective. The question is no longer what the pupils are doing to the thickets and the barrow but what the thickets and barrow are doing to the pupils. If we want to look forward and consider what this story might mean for sustainable education in the future, we must appreciate what it is these young people have learnt through their participation and their experience: their feelings about and understanding of the barrow have changed! They know it much better now for the simple reason that they have stood and walked on it – it has become an experience. Their senses make associations through all they have seen, heard, smelt, touched. The barrow has become a sensory experience to which ideas can be attached. And thanks to the pupils' work it has become something more. Everything you work on, everything that you shape by your actions, you are *connected to*, for you have invested a part of yourself in it. It is through active work with nature that human beings enter into and claim their own relationship to it (Krogh 2010). In such a work session it's as if the barrow has become theirs, for as Greve (2005) writes, the world about us reaches deep and far into our inner life. In this way, the barrow and the pupils are woven together. Naturally, through meaningful work.

The fjord: place for rowing and fishing

The learning arena

Stretched out, Norway's coastline is over 80,000 km long – long enough to go twice around the earth! A large part of the country's settled area was traditionally tied to sea and fjord, both to access the oceans' and rivers' resources and as the most effective means of travelling long distances. The coastal communities have always had close contact with the rest of Europe. The story of the coastal culture and tales about the ocean's fabulous bounty are largely synonymous with Norway's history. The biodiversity in the sea and along the coast is enormous and far from fully explored. Traditions associated with boat-building, fishing and cargo shipping are alive and well and can easily be made accessible to pupils. Indre Sogn kystlag (coastal association) arranges activities in and around the fjord. They own, maintain and operate several so-called Sogne boats, hold courses and lectures and organize social gatherings.[4] They collaborate with the Norwegian Trekking Association, Kystled Nærøyfjorden (see box) and all the municipalities in Indre Sogn.

For those navigating the fjord by paddle or sail, Indre Sogn's coastal association has built a network of overnight accommodation. This network is called Kystled Nærøyfjord. The coastal association owns three Sogne boats, which can be hired at a reasonable rate. With a good old-fashioned rowing boat and simple lodgings you can experience the fjord landscape in Aurland municipality in an environmentally friendly way. For more information about boat hire, accommodation, maps of the area and useful links, see: http://kystled-sogn.no/

Underway with the coastal association, in cooperation with the Children's Hiking Association and the Nature Inspectorate (SNO). Photograph: SNO

Enactment analysis

The instant we step into a rowing boat, we are in an arena that requires us to learn to move in relation to something that is always moving; to find our sea legs, that is, to be able to board and land with a flow that the boat's movements demand of us. If someone wants to move when we are all on board, they can only do so if the others sit still. We are literally in the same boat. Learning to row is, again, a matter of finding a flow in the movement of the oars, in their simple, repeated strokes. Rowing is thus extremely simple – yet sophisticated. The whole body must be tuned to the stroke of the oars, and at the same time must adjust to the movement and waves the boat is subjected to. To row, in other words, is to learn to be limber, adaptive, and present in all these movements.

The act of adjusting to the material we are working with is something that rowing has in common with handicrafts. Whoever masters a craft is present with all their attention in an extended 'body' that the interaction with the material generates. For instance, a glassblower is connected to all the movements in their molten material – and their thoughts must stay attentive and alert to be able to act with assurance and at the right instant.

The next skill to learn is rowing together. The person sitting at the front of the boat has no choice but to follow the pace and rhythm of the person further back (who is facing away from them). At the same time, both rowers must be in contact with each other and notice when there is flow in the strokes they pull together. A finer form of silent interaction and teamwork is hard to find. Further, as with all handicraft, *the feedback comes from the encounter with the material itself.* This means the work is 'self-instructing' – teachers don't need to admonish pupils to work together one way or another. To find flow in the boat, pupils have to find flow in their interaction.

The river: place for ecological awareness

The river as ecosystem

The river is its own master. It is full of energy and finds its own way to the sea. At the same time, the river is fickle, responsive to any change. The rivers in Western Norway and in the mountains rush over waterfalls and through narrow glens into tranquil valley plains, while the rivers inland and northwards up to Finnmark are wider, more sedate and navigable by boat. The landscape's character is reflected in the character of the river.

The river is an important ecosystem with a rich diversity of plants, insects and animals tied to it, and it gives life and nourishment to agricultural areas in the valleys and plains it runs through. The energy of the river has made it possible to grind grain into flour and to saw timber into planks. It is used to produce electricity which is sent to towns far away. The river draws the attention of people of all ages and offers a host of activities and experiences: play with bark boats and sticks, and many types of rod fishing. The sound of running water fills the landscape and creates a sense of space.

The Tokvam brook

In autumn 2011, the head of the local river owners' association contacted ABU with a suggestion for teaching plans and tasks involving the school in a research project about the trout of the Aurland river. This project has now been running for three years and starts in Class 1.

Class 2 are having an outdoor day. They're helping to make the Aurland river more attractive to fish. The river has already been replenished with gravel and stone. Trout and salmon need this on the river bed to spawn, and the young fish need hiding places to shelter in while they are growing up. The pupils have watched videos from the river of trout sculpting nests in the gravel. They have seen them spawning and how the female uses her tail to scoop gravel over the fertilized eggs. They have learnt about the trout's migration out to the sea and the dangers awaiting them there (including the salmon louse), as well as threats inland along rivers and streams. When people clear land along watercourses they remove trees, making it difficult for fish to find cover from predators. This is something that the pupils can help to remedy. Today they've gone up to Tokvam brook to build hiding places for the fish. They saw down trees and branches and place them in the stream. They help to plant willows along the banks. The pupils are keen and work hard even though it's been raining all day. In autumn they will go upriver and see if their efforts have paid off and there are more fish.

On the school's website we read under Class 3 news (2014):

Researchers and anglers visit

How fares our trout Teo? Is he alive? Where is he now? Is he still in the river or has he travelled out into the wide blue yonder? Class 3 had many questions when the researchers from the Norwegian Institute for Water Research (NIVA) visited on Monday. Finally, we would hear about Teo and the other trout we helped tag in the spring. Happily, the news was good. Teo has eluded the seals and fishermen and is alive and well. After his release, he travelled down the river and out into the fjord. It's likely he made a trip further out. The researchers said that one of the trout they tagged had swum quite a distance – making it all the way out to the open sea. Many of the other tagged fish had stayed in the local area. They had swum up to the lake, where they seem to be doing well. Teo's battery will last a year, so we wait with bated breath for new signs of life. On Monday we learnt about the work being done to help the trout in the river. According to the divers there are more trout in the river now than for quite some time. The pupils were also visited by two anglers who have fished in the river since they were small. They taught us a lot about fly fishing. We got to see how a mayfly is tied and afterwards we learnt how to cast with a fly rod on the playing field. It was really fun!

Enactment analysis

That thoughts can *wander beyond what we can see* in our immediate surroundings, that they can *wait for what is not yet there*, keep on wondering over a period of time – these are two traits of exploratory thinking. We don't yet have the answer in our grasp and so we have to be attentive to which direction the enquiry will go. When we focus our attention on something, our thoughts are alert and really concentrated on that thing. When the pupils are with the researchers implanting a transmitter, they focus attention on Teo. We put a tag on the trout to follow him over time. The pupils take notice of this. Indeed, the longer the exercise continues and the more they see the operation as a complete event, the harder it is for them to simply forget Teo and his tag. In the fleeting instant he is released and vanishes *out of sight*, he does not disappear *out of mind*. Where he is headed is a question written in the river and fjord, a riddle whose answer everyone naturally wants to know. Without giving the pupils any prompts on an activity sheet, the exercise has spawned a research question that the class, together with the researchers, have connected to and can experience for a whole year – as long as Teo's battery lasts.

The mountains: place for resources and recreation

The learning arena

Norway is a mountainous country, with large tracts of land stretching out above the tree-line. The mountains are frequented in both summer and winter, but excursions there require sound planning and skill in assessing safety and the changing weather conditions. The mountains represent an utterly open space, where we come near the light and the sky above us. The terrain and nature may seem uniform, but look closer and you'll see a great variety of vegetation, colours, patterns and fauna. Many mountain lakes are rich in fish. Since vegetation appears so late in high mountain areas, much of the natural and cultural history is easy to spot and to read: scree and glacial boulders from the ice age, and reindeer pitfall traps and stone hides dating back to when the first human communities came here.

Fishing day in the mountains

In the autumn, often in late August, rangers from the Mountain Ranger Office make their way into the mountains and set nets in waters where they know there are fish. The following day, school classes come to draw up the nets. The day is well planned. The pupils get to row the boat, haul in the net, gut and clean the fish, salt them, light a fire and cook the fish on a hot stone over it. In lower secondary school, classes can join rangers at one of their stations, set nets, stay overnight and haul in the catch early next morning. Then they join in the test fishing, measuring and weighing the fish, and investigate how the lake should be managed and cultivated in the future.

The lower secondary school classes are active in the mountain landscape in many ways. They bike the Navvy Road along the railway line, walk the Aurland Valley and follow the old drovers' roads from glacier to fjord. They have a partnership agreement with a local hotel, helping to produce local food for its restaurant. In this way the pupils progressively develop their understanding of the industries in the area. They participate in production that hinges on the use of local resources. They take on a range of tasks and form relationships with people and places across the district. With time, more businesses have become involved in the scheme. Pupils have studied local foodcraft and hosted tour-

Mountain fishing. Photograph: Aurland fjellstyre

On the way to Melane. Photo: ABU

Measuring and weighing the fish. Photograph: ABU

Making ready the packhorse, Class 9. Steiner school at Skjold. Photograph: Jorunn Barane

ist outings on the fjord. The school also offers a course in local guiding on which pupils learn the best ways to communicate a place.

Enactment analysis

In the mountains we climb from the valley to find views and perspective. The forces we meet up here are quite unlike those down in the infields and on the farm. Here, weather and wind rule and we must learn to live with the seasons and forces of nature – to open a form of dialogue with them through our responses to the shifting weather and situations. In the great outdoors the pupils encounter a high degree of external resistance. It is a demanding environment.

On the other hand, the mountains can feel freer than the space we normally inhabit between school, shops and petrol station. Up here, we must stand tall and face the elements and learn to be on familiar terms with this space. Out of this comes a sense of mastery and an expanded sense of what 'at home' can mean. To feel at home in the midst of these forces, to know them across different terrain and seasons – this is something children and young people need the opportunity to learn. The Norwegian concept of friluftsliv, literally 'free air life', tries to capture all of these dimensions: a life that is free in an air that is free. The pupils' exposure to stewardship tasks when they assist the Mountain Ranger Office with their test fishing builds a bridge between outdoor recreation and nature management. Working with professionals who have the mountains and fishing as their daily work expands their understanding of what constitutes their own space. With this expansion of school into the wide open spaces the pupils grow and glimpse their own place in relation to a larger and broader landscape. They see routes and connections between other districts and regions, and old routes and works that have fallen out of use, their story spelled out on the landscape – a story it is the district's duty to pass on. Outdoor life and fishing in mountain lakes extends pupils' relationship to the place they have grown up in – and leads them into a role of stewardship. One can always come back to what one loves. No matter where one is in the world, it will be like an anchor, a universal home – which, although place-bound, feels infinite. Mountain and fjord are thus open spaces, spaces that make room for everyone regardless of which valley they come from.

When we meet other people in the mountains, we can also feel something of the same openness in the encounter. We connect in our experiences of the elements, and nature brings us together.

In rough terrain and changing weather situations young people will recognize the authority and leadership that lie not so much in bossing others around as in grounded experience in how to keep safe, find the path, stay warm and keep the team together. Their recognition and appreciation of natural authority tends to surface when exposed to challenging situations. The mountain is a space where you meet challenges and overcome your limits. But you need safe guidance as well, and learn to appreciate it. Outdoor recreation and mountain life provide a unique arena in which to guide pupils into such transformative experiences without compromising our responsibility as schools or teachers. Looking back on them, the pupils love these challenges, which bring together people of all backgrounds and ages. Warmth and food are never better than when we've been cold and hungry; rest never feels better than when we are exhausted. We come home to the familiar and appreciate the things we might otherwise take for granted.

The wider world: the space of human ecology

Act locally

In the early 2000s, a reception centre for asylum-seekers opened in Aurland. A group of teenagers from Albania, Somalia and Iran living there had Norwegian lessons at the agricultural college. We offered them practical experience in the fields, the greenhouse and the workshop. Afterwards we took them to the classroom to reflect, write about what they'd done, and talk. In the course of this we picked up poems and stories from them – including the stories that had brought them to Norway. This made a deep impression on us. 'I'm still too young to look after my family', said the 16-year-old from Iran who had come to Norway with his mother and sister. They had heard no news of the father. He had disappeared.

We saw a correlation between the youths' connecting to the place they had come to and their learning of its language. They entered into a community with the other pupils and staff and became part of a social context. Not least, they had something to do while they waited for their applications to be processed. It was also a time of laughter and joy. It was important to find humour in simple things, in the here and now. The teenagers often referred to their own countries and their home surroundings there. All had experience of growing food on allotments. They had weeded and handled vegetables from an early age, so gardening was nothing new and gave us a common frame of reference – even if the boys sometimes dropped hints that this was women's work, and low status. The

Sale of products made by the pupils. Photograph: ABU

18-year-old from Somalia composed a story about his homeland which he presented in Norwegian to Class 12 at the school. This was cultural exchange at its best, even if it was no easy task to talk about a country facing such great challenges. It was plain that integration and language learning are influenced by support, relationships and shared frames of reference. These years with the municipal reception centre brought positive experiences for the district and the school. Helping others enhances our lives.

> New arrivals integrate more easily into our society when the unspoken features of our culture are made clear to them. (NCC 1997, p. 16)

The outermost circle in the Aurland model involves engagement and solidarity with the wider world. The school actively encourages entrepreneurship and solidarity in the learning environment. The kindergarten and pupils in several year groups build their own businesses and sell their products to support different solidarity projects. From the district they reach out to the world with an understanding that is based on tasks they have participated in locally. An example is Nina Children Home in Kenya. Nina has connections to the village and she has visited the school and other venues in the community to present her project.

This is what we in Aurland call a 'place-based sustainable learning path'. Such a learning path can be developed anywhere using the cultural and natural resources locally available. The Aurland model shows how businesses, voluntary organizations and public institutions can partner with the school to make an integrated learning environment where the municipality as a whole forms the learning arena. Curricula have been located in the landscape from fjord to mountain. Using local resources, making visible the path from earth and fjord to table, developing appreciation and respect for, and knowledge of, the diverse natural resource base – these lie at the heart of the learning. Through place-based activities, pupils gain mastery through the use of body and senses. As their activities extend out into the landscape, their sense of *belonging* develops – a capacity that can be transferred to other places. Key principles are experiential learning, exploratory work methods, cross-disciplinary collaboration and project work in which the development of *entrepreneurship* is central (Krogh 2010).

The last few years have seen efforts to expand the local curriculum to include the whole of Aurland municipality as a learning arena for classes both from local schools and from further afield. Science and social studies, and especially 'food and health', underpin the teaching plans. Topics like ecology, ethical animal husbandry, environment and sustainable learning are also covered. SJH and ABU have collaborated with the municipality and various of the district's volunteer organizations and businesses. This broad partnership rests on a shared commitment to sustainable development.

How to make the outermost circle in the model the 'wider world'? Can we train ourselves to think globally and thereby broaden our perspective? We must lift our gaze, learn to see our place in the world in solidarity with other cultures and peoples. This means expanding our self – understanding ourselves as part of a larger context, which Arne Næss calls 'the extended self' (Haukeland 2008).

Think globally, act locally

The globe is an interwoven civilization; we coalesce in a common destiny. This has many benefits but it also means each problem is global and concerns all of us. If we confront children and young people with the suffering in the world, it is our duty to contribute to positive action, so that our pupils will also experience a sense of possibility and hope. Hope is a driving force, a motivator; it influences the will and gives us the strength to master what is yet to be. Hope is a mission. It is among the key life skills to which all school subjects should contribute.

Teaching may be informed by respect for the greatness of nature and for the distinctive character of different cultures, what the Czech playwright and statesman Vaclav Havel – speaking of hope – called 'the great and mysterious order of Being', where everything has a place of its own and nothing that has once been done can be undone; where in some unfathomable way it is recorded for eternity (Havel 2004). Advocates of transformative learning also challenge us to think big, to expand our understanding of ourselves and our place in the modern world. As well as education for *planetary awareness*, for *integrated development*, for *quality of life*, this involves a restoration of 'mystery' and our curiosity towards it (Jacobsen 2005, p. 245). According to the philosopher Trond Gansmo Jakobsen, this larger narrative might include a story about how the universe evolved, how life originated and how humankind is a product of these processes. It should take us back into the nature and world that created us (ibid., p. 246), showing us that we have a universal responsibility and a place in both the local and the global community (ibid., p. 11).

Recent theories of place identity presume that it is not immutable and static, but rather is constantly evolving (Massey 1997). Identity is place based but not place bound. This means it is also shaped by external, global processes and not solely the result of local experiences. Both sense of place and identity with place can therefore be understood as ambiguous and 'glocal'. We should be open to and tolerant of cultural differences instead of putting up social and mental walls around 'our place'. We must accept and applaud the fact that the global and local are woven together like warp and woof, that we live in a world where impulses and influences go in all directions.

Human ecology

Jakobsen writes (2005, p. 218) that an ecologically oriented understanding means thinking and behaving in the knowledge that we are part of a system of relationships and processes – the fabric of life – and that we have a common destiny with the other beings who share this planet with us. We cannot detach our knowledge from our surroundings. Ethical questions depend, for better or worse, on our situation, so we feel our way through life, making new tracks in uncharted terrain based on what we believe is right and best. This means that, though ethical principles can rest on individual values (ibid., p. 228), they must also be linked to systems and holistic thinking, embedded in relationships. We must be open to change and adjustment because the world around us is changing. Jakobsen also says that the goal of ethics is not finite and certain, but a process of working creatively, imaginatively and as an intermediary in disputes where ethical questions are at stake. 'Our surroundings are just as much a part of us as we are part of our surroundings' (ibid., p. 230). Seen this way, all our surroundings are important – urban areas, wilderness, parks, towns, seas, steppes, forests, farmland and mountains.

Institutions (like schools), organizations and cultural systems must be constantly reassessed. Values change too, and we need to be receptive to transformation and growth. In the future we must be prepared to tackle the unforeseeable, the new and the immutable in a complex and uncertain world. Children and young people should not be raised to meet society as it is now; they should be equipped to shape society in the future, independently and inventively. The role of knowledge, then, is to help children orientate themselves in the world, and give them the courage and insight to change it.

Furthermore, the individual in each child must be shown a way towards ethical action and personal development. The objective of pedagogy has to be to create the best possible conditions for this innermost and, in the deepest sense, sacred part of the person to come into its own. How can parents and teachers prepare the way for children and young people to grow fully into *their* own distinctive being? How can we enable every single pupil to find their purpose, develop their abilities, and fulfil their academic, social and cultural potential? The source of innovation, creativity and, with them, human development lies latent in our own individual being in connection with our surroundings. To lead people to this source is therefore to show them the way towards educating themselves. Thereby, teaching becomes a process also of fostering children's emotional life.

A way to help pupils find the answers in themselves is through dialogic questioning. Here, rather than 'putting things into' consciousness, the goal is to help them 'make the subconscious conscious and the implicit explicit' (Østergaard 2004). Authentic, open-ended questions give them the chance to contribute their own comments and suggestions. Their interpretation and understanding are not something the teacher can predict in advance, and authentic questions signal that their contribution is important. It follows that the teacher also has to follow up questions from students and build on what they have to say. There will be no real dialogue unless the teacher appreciates pupils as a source of knowledge and takes their replies seriously.

What's often absent from educational theories is deeper engagement and reflection about what place the human being has in a larger cosmological and ecological context. We have forgotten that all of our learning and all of our actions are closely connected to the world that has given us life. As Jakobsen says, we must switch our focus towards this ecological community if we are to find ourselves again (2005, p. 1): 'We must change the way we think and act. We must understand that we are part of a larger community of life. We must reorient ourselves towards an "ideal of community with the earth". Planet Earth must be our teacher.'

Seven aspects of unfolding potential

The Norwegian primary and lower secondary education system was reformed in 1997 and a new curriculum was implemented. Building on the humanistic ideals of European educational philosophy, it centres on the human being and 'the unfolding of its potential'. Everything is geared towards enabling the versatile development of individual qualities and skills. These are grouped in the curriculum into seven aspects of unfolding human potential, namely:

1. human seeking of meaning;
2. human creativivity;
3. human knowing;
4. human work;
5. human collaboration;
6. environmental and nature awareness;
7. human integrity.

The unfolding of these capacities requires real-life contexts that can awaken the will to act.

Responsibility and autonomy

Every child is born with an innate interest in, curiosity about and openness to its surroundings. From early childhood on, we connect to and build lasting bonds with our human and natural environment. This first process builds our sense of belonging, which is a premise and promise for *growing responsibility*: what we feel connected to, we may also feel responsible for. A second process starts in individual participation and leads to individual skills, capacities and sensitivities as a basis for independent thinking, judgement and ethical action. This process builds our sense of self, which is the promise for *growing autonomy*. To really understand how these two senses serve each other, we must learn to see how they coevolve.

In any encounter with the world a double process takes place. On one hand, we have a potential to *be moved* by what we meet, whether it be a landscape, a human being or an animal. Someone or something moves us, resonates in us. In any situation involving the senses, this potential exists. On the other hand, an encounter with the world can *set something in us in motion*: an inner movement of wonder, of thought or emotion, of language or deed. A part of us can take part in the world. Through this double process of receptivity and participation, we develop skills and capacities. And as capacities and skills grow, our ability to let the world speak to us and become part of us grows too.

The secret of place-based education is that these two processes are seen as inseparable. In Part II we shall explore in more detail aspects of these double processes and what it means to connect them. Each of the seven aspects we explore reveals a different variation of this main theme.

PART II

IDENTITY AND SUSTAINABILITY: SEVEN ASPECTS OF UNFOLDING POTENTIAL

Nikolai Astrup. Rhubarb, 1928. Photograph ©: O. Væring Eftf. AS

The circle must be made

A central motif in Nicolai Astrup's (1880–1928) art is the relationship between people and place (Haugsbø 2011). He expresses this theme using colour, brushwork and the West Norwegian landscape. In the painting of rhubarb-picking in a garden, we can see how much the human presence matters to Astrup. It is people who create life from nature and make nature their own through their interactions with it. The dress worn by Engel, Astrup's wife, gives coherence and balance to the picture. Together with the blossoming apple tree on the left and the snow-capped mountain in the background, Engel in her pale rose-patterned dress completes a *circle*, perhaps life's circle. A connection is made between the human and nature, between the garden and the distant mountain. The circle mediates between natural and human worlds and represents here a circle of everyday life. In the garden fundamental values can also be cultivated. Local and global circles must constantly be made and expressed afresh. They are never completed once and for all.

Language, landscape and stories

To understand the origin of our language is in essence a matter of learning that stories are inherent in the landscape and in nature and in human interaction with them. To hear and tell stories is a unique way to increase our understanding of ourselves as individual human beings but also as part of a wider interwoven community of people, nature and culture (Gersie et al. 2014). Storytelling is a powerful tool to integrate and communicate various dimensions of culture and heritage within a common place-based context.

Oral narrative is also a way of voicing, speaking into action, supporting and shaping in words the changes one wishes to see in the world. To create what is not yet there, as inward images, and to express them through stories can light the way towards both an individual and a social, sustainable future. A storyteller can make available to pupils stories of the interplay between nature, humanity and culture.

Language, landscape and thought

The Austrian philosopher Ludwig Wittgenstein (1889–1951) kept his favourite writing hut in Skjolden, a village in Luster in Sogn. It was here that he wrote his most famous works. Wittgenstein believed there was an important relationship between thinking and language, and between language, landscape and forms of life. The traditional problems of philosophy are born of insufficient attention to the connection between language use and forms of life or ways of living, he says. Separating words and concepts from their natural and living contexts results in the 'idling' of language (Dahlin 2004).

The premise is that all knowledge about the vital questions of existence, all life skills and wisdom, are by their nature embedded in actual situations and practices, since it is here that they find expression (ibid., p.5). With this in mind, how do we prevent environmental education becoming mere empty words? How to connect it to life so that it stops 'idling', and engages? The answer has two parts. The first concerns *learning arenas*.

When learning is authentically situated (Lave and Wenger 1991) or contextualized (Nordal 2006), then language and thoughts gain external purchase in the world. The second is the *learning approach*. When teaching methods have variety as well as depth, employing hand as well as feeling, then budding knowledge and language are internally rooted in our own body, feeling and form of life.

We begin with a story from our local history and a trip out along the Sognefjord, all the way out, and north to Selja on the Stadlandet peninsula, home to the legend of St Sunniva.

Boat trip route between Aurland and Selje. Map: Masaoki Adachi

CHAPTER FOUR

SEEKING MEANING

How can nature and landscape help us to teach about religion and world views? Can stories and first-hand experience spark pupils' interest to look deeper into nature and themselves and so make new connections? We were inspired to work with the Celtic legend of St Sunniva from Selja. Before we could learn about Sunniva we needed to understand something of the distinctive nature of Celtic Christianity. Our source was Olav Stokland's (1969) book on Norway's inner history, *Av Norges indre historie*.

The legend of St Sunniva

Sunniva was the daughter of an Irish king and part of the group of peoples we call Celts. In the eighth century BC in the early Iron Age, the Celts crossed the sea from continental Europe to the British Isles and Ireland. Surviving legends and sagas about the Emerald Isle in the Western Sea lend Ireland a paradisal quality. The Celtic gods were formed by the red light of dawn and the afterglow in the evening sky, by moonlight silver and the starry heavens. At sacred sites, temples could consist of a simple stone circle whose walls were clouds on the horizon and whose roof was the blue canopy of the heavens. In sight of the sea with all its shifting moods, people learnt to hear nature speak. When Christianity arrived, the Celts felt that it came for nature's sake as well as for humankind's. Christ was in his death and ascension like an inner sun in the human heart, a notion that became embodied in the Celtic cross. Softly in the multitude we hear Sunniva, the voice of a Christianity directed towards human beings' inner nature.

> Sunniva means the 'hidden sun' she bore her child in our hearts and whoever nurtures this inner child shall never walk alone, not even in the darkest night. (Stokland 1969, p.72)

During the spring, Class 3 had a unit on Sunniva of Selja. It was a warm meeting with the Irish saint. After the summer holidays the teacher wanted to start the school year with a trip. With the story still fresh on their minds the children decided, 'We're going to Selja!' By boat we would travel all the way out and get to view our district from the sea. Our home lies in the innermost reach of the longest fjord in the world, 200 km long. Not far to the north lies Selja island, where the legend endures to this day (see the map on p. 65). The fjord was the region's most important traffic artery, before today's roads and tunnels through the mountains. After a week spent working with the topic in the classroom, we made for the place where the story belongs.

The way out to Selja

So, one day in August, 20 pupils are standing at the quay at the head of our fjord, waving to their parents. It is half past five in the morning. As we pass the narrow Nærøyfjord, we see the sun dancing red and orange on the high mountain peaks. We know we are heading for the light and the horizon. Further out, the landscape opens up, the mountains become gentler and the orchards slope down prettily to the water. We land at Balestrand to change boats. The catamaran Sognekongen will take us the next leg, and we have breakfast on board. At last we can see the horizon. We enjoy the sea views and the warm weather and spend most of the trip on deck. At Solund island we have to change boats again. One goes west to Bergen, while ours heads north to the settlement of Selje. By now most of us are in unfamiliar waters. We are in the archipelago, passing islands with names like Svanøy, Askvoll and Måløy. We sail past Hornelen, a cliff jutting straight out of the sea. Over 800 m high, it has long been a landmark to steer by. Excitement mounts among the pupils. Where is Selja? Is it the island over there?

One of the parents with us grew up in Selje municipality. She is acting as our guide and speaks warmly of her home landscape, which is looking its very best today. Finally we glimpse the little island to our west. Reaching Selje harbour, we unload our baggage. A smaller boat and guide wait to take us out to Selja. 'Can we dress up now?', asks one of the girls. Some of us change into dresses and other finery and we are ready for Sunniva and the abbey ruins. It takes 15 minutes around the headland before we catch sight of the clock tower and abbey. The guide leads us up a path and into the atrium, where we sit on benches in what was once a rose garden. Now he begins to speak, and we hear the story of Sunniva one more time.

The story of Sunniva, about 1000 years ago

In one of Ireland's many kingdoms there lived a good king with a daughter whose name was Sunniva. The king ruled his country well, and after he died his daughter inherited the kingdom. She had been raised in the Christian faith and she set an example for others to follow. Rumours of Sunniva's good deeds and devout ways spread far and wide. In one of the neighbouring kingdoms a Viking king ruled. He used force to subdue his people and to satisfy his every wish. When he heard about Sunniva and her goodness he wanted her for his wife. He both enticed and threatened her. She would get all she wanted if she married him, but if she refused he would kill everyone in her land and lay it waste. But Sunniva had made a sacred vow to serve Christ all her life. She would rather flee the land than marry a tyrant.

Sunniva and her companions took to three ships. They set out to sea without sails and without oars, putting their fate in God's hands. Wind and currents took them to the Norwegian coast. One of the ships ran aground on the island of Kinn, while Sunniva and her companions were led to Selja. Here they settled in a cave they found among the rocks at the island's edge. They lived simply and served God in prayer and song. They lived on fish from the sea and fruit, berries and roots. Now the island was also used by others for grazing sheep and goats. It happened that some of the animals went missing, as they still do today when they're left unshepherded. But the Norwegians on the mainland accused Sunniva and her companions of stealing.

Sunniva of Selja

These farmers went to the jarl in Nidaros and asked him to come with ships and men to seize the Christians and kill them. Sunniva and her people then hid in a cavern beneath a crag. They asked God to save them from the heathens. Sunniva gathered everyone in prayer. She prayed that the cave would collapse and cover their bodies. All at once there was a great bang and the mountain crashed over them. Their prayers had been answered.

One evening, a ship of traders was sailing past Selja when suddenly they saw a column of light shining from the island. Going ashore to investigate, they found on the beach a skull that smelled fragrant and beamed with light. Even though they were heathens they wrapped the skull in a clean cloth and took it north with them to Nidaros. Bishop Sigurd realized that the skull must be from a holy person. He asked Olav Tryggvason, the King, to travel to Selja. On the western side of the island, facing the sea, they found the cave that had collapsed. Inside they discovered the bones and remains of the Selja people. Finally, they discovered Sunniva. Her body was unscathed and she looked like she was sleeping. It was clear to all that she was a holy person. King Olav had a church erected outside the cave. They placed the holy Sunniva in a fine chest, to make a shrine.

Swept up in the story, we can see the high wall remaining from the Sunniva and also the crypt where the shrine stood before the Bishop took it to Bergen when he left Selja. The shrine was placed with great honour on the high altar in Christ Church in Bergen on 7 September 1170.

We climb the long steep stone stairway to Michael's Cave; we pick flowers and lay them on the modest stone altar. This is the oldest sanctified place in Norway. According to legend, it was Archangel Michael who heard Sunniva's prayer and caused the cave to collapse. Further down the slope we find Sunniva Spring, a small stream forming a pool. We drink the pure water, which is said to have healing properties – the children are convinced of it. After a short crabbing expedition on the shore we cross to the shallow white beach on the mainland. There we cook and stay the rest of the day, swimming, and digging in the sand. In the evening the children learn the song 'The Sun Is Setting' as the great, red ball of the sun sets on the horizon. All this in one day. We spend the night in classrooms at the local school.

Homeward and inward: seeing oneself from the outside

Do the historical events connected with Selja have anything to do with its topography and location? Was it merely a coincidence that the Christian impulse from Ireland landed exactly here? Does landscape have a latent potential that we humans can help to release?

It's time to leave the sea behind for now and head home, back into the Sognefjord. The further in we come, the narrower and tighter it gets, and we are impressed how the sea can push so far in between high mountains and glaciers to meet the lush orchards. Furthest in lies our home: it's almost like living in a cave. Heading homewards and inwards we see our own place from outside, which leads us to ask: What lies hidden in our own landscape that we can bring forth and encourage? What does our place have that no other place has? What relationships and contexts are we part of? When we come home again from the fjord or the mountains, many of us feel that we see it from a new perspective and in a bigger context. Who knows, we may even have our very own local St Sunniva. Here is her story.

The story of Aud the Deep-Minded

A 'queen's grave' was unearthed by the fjord on Vinjum farm in Aurland. The finds are now housed in the Historic Museum in Bergen. The grave contained a woman lying in a ship. In life she must have been powerful – she wore a belt holding keys to all the doors on her estate, and around her was everything she needed for her life after death: tools, jewellery and incense burners finely ornamented in the Celtic style.

The grave evokes the story of Aud the Deep-Minded, who came from Kvam farm in Aurland (Hvammur in Old Norse). Aud was married to Olaf the White in Ireland. After he was killed in battle she fled to Iceland, where she began to spread the Christianity she had learnt in Ireland. She named her Icelandic home Hvammur, and the farm still lies at Hvammsfjord. When she died she was buried under the rocks on the shore so the waves washing over her would connect her to the land of her birth (Ohnstad 1991). If you ask Icelanders today about Aud the Deep-Minded, many will be familiar with her story and the place where she lived.

So why set out on a journey? Bo Dahlin (2010) gives the following answer: 'To live is to wander life's path. To follow a path is to travel. Travelling, as we are all aware, gives us stories to tell. Stories are in themselves a way of journeying through symbolic landscapes.' (2010, pp. 166–179)

To shift perspective, change our viewpoint and take part in others' mental journeys, this is the nature of language; of what connects the telling and the listening. Sharing a story is sharing a movement of soul (Hugo 1995). It is a way to move our thinking and emotion to partake in each other's lives. By developing language and by listening to stories we become able to step outside our own point of view and see and experience things as others might experience and see them, and thereby be moved.

The stories in Part I tie the concept of *sustainable learning* to this inner and outer movement, where the goal is to be able to see and understand both from without and from within. Using the Aurland model, we have shown how local curricula can transport pupils between different viewpoints in the landscape and in natural and cultural history. The pupils also alternate between being the *finders* and *creators* of stories. Through participation in shaping the same landscape they learn to write themselves into the grand narrative that place and history ultimately are. To change point of view, to travel, to shift perspective – these are the methods available to us in our searching. When we move between different places, a question naturally arises of what connects them. To come home is, in life as in understanding, to become that bridge which connects one place with the other.

FOR REFLECTION:

As a teacher ask yourself: What is the goal of going on a school trip?

Identity in the meeting with the world and each other

Intellectual freedom implies not only allowance for other points of view, but also courage to take a stand, confidence to stand alone, and the strength of character to think and act according to one's own convictions (NCC 1997, p. 4).

In the book *Transformative Learning and Identity* (Illeris 2013) a social theory of learning is introduced, that is, a theory about social participation as a path of learning and understanding. Here, identity is one of the central components of learning, together with meaning, practice and community. Identity grows as a social dimension: we define who we are by how we experience ourselves through both participation and membership in a community. But identity also grows as a learning trajectory: we define who we are by where we have been and where we are going. Further, Illeris casts identity both as a nexus of multiple membership and as a relationship between the local and the global (Illeris 2013, p. 91). Hjalmar Hegge (1989) shows how from antiquity the cultural history of the West is the story of the gradual emergence of human individuality and freedom. At the same time, he argues, this idea of human freedom is impossible to conceive or fulfil in isolation because it is inextricably linked to the development of a new sociality in people's interactions with the world and each other. In the book *Å finne sted* [Taking Place] Førde and colleagues (2013) argue that identity is or may be the way we are present in the world, the way we experience it in the here and now – the relations, dialogue and attachments we have with our surroundings, other people and ourselves. Our sense of identity and belonging is constantly in movement, based on the experience and history of the society we live in and of ourselves and others; they are in dialogue with who we are, our feelings, our self-image and how secure and dependent we are in our relations with others (Førde et al. 2013).

When the individual's self-esteem awakens it becomes an important source of inspiration and the spur of many biographies of people who go their own way, find their own voice and make their own mark in the world. Such stories can be found in the world at large, but also on our doorstep. One example is the artist Johannes Vinjum, who found his voice through the visual arts after travelling in the world and while abroad saw his own locality from the outside.

Into the world to find oneself

Johannes Vinjum (1930–92) was from Aurland. After art school in Oslo, he was awarded a Thomas Fearnley grant. He bought a scooter and travelled around Spain and France, where he immersed himself in art and architecture. His travels took him to Chartres, the city with the famous cathedral. These duly became his city and his cathedral, to which he would return regularly. The wanderlust had taken hold, as for so many coastal people before him. Vinjum thought this had to do with the seaway to the west. He saw the Sognefjord as the autostrada to the world beyond, a connection he believed was a significant part of this region's cultural history (Vinjum 2009, p. 303).

Yes, Vinjum was an inveterate traveller. 'But,' he says, 'I must return to Aurland and the Sognefjord. Often. And to the Continent – to Chartres and the cathedral. Perhaps there's a connection: the monumentality and the dimensions set against man's smallness; the mountains rising up from the fjord, the soaring cathedral. The Gothic seeks a universe. For me, these themes touch on something divine, boundary-breaking, something mystical. Something I am drawn to.' (ibid. p. 304) Harald Flor (1982) says that Vinjum accentuates the monumental effect using thick, painstakingly built-up layers of paint, while his nuanced palette captures the immediacy of experience, the myriad complementary tones awakening associations with the colour play of the cathedral's interior.

Such dimensions make us aware of our own tininess, yet the rock formations rising up along the fjord are familiar and much liked. They convey not oppressive remoteness, but affinity. Houses and boathouses stand as though grown from the landscape, built with materials from nature and weathered by the same inhospitable forces.

Johannes Vinjum, untitled. © Johannes Vinjum/ BONO 2015. Photograph©: O. Væring Eftf. AS. [West portal of Chartres Cathedral]

Johannes Vinjum, Winter's day, Aurland , 1975. © Johannes Vinjum/ BONO 2015. Photograph©: O. Væring Eftf. AS

Fog doesn't always weigh down on the Sognfjell peaks, as we can see in this painting, an intense, luminous picture from the late 1970s (Flor 1982).

For reflection:

If you were to travel somewhere in order to come back and see your home with new eyes, where would you go?

CHAPTER FIVE

CREATIVITY

The faculty of imagining

> Imagination … is the most accurate and truth-telling faculty which the human mind possesses. – Zarathustra (Surti 1981, p. 36)

One Sunday a leg of lamb lay thawing on the kitchen worktop. The seven-year-old happened upon what was lying there and started to tell a story. On the spot, she created the lamb's story from this frozen joint. Just like that, she raised the lamb up on its four legs, gave it flesh and blood and made it breathe again. We could almost see it moving and grazing on the green slopes. 'I feel sorry for it, but I still eat meat.' She talked at length about keeping farm animals and why we must slaughter them. She shared her reflections on life and death and the fact that we will all die someday. She examined the meat and found a loose bone: 'Look! It has loose teeth, just like I do.'

'You know so much!', I said.

Why yes, she had learnt it in Spiren kindergarten, where she had followed the sheep through the year.

'What do *you* learn at school, then?'

'Um. Don't know, really … counting and spelling …'

> Fairy tales are stories that make no claim to be true. Albert Einstein was a great advocate of fairy tales. A concerned mother once visited him to seek his advice on how to help her son become a maths whizz. Exactly what should she read to her son to best prepare him for a career as a brilliant scientist? 'Fairy tales,' said Einstein.
>
> 'Okay', said the mother, 'and after that?'
>
> 'More fairy tales', said Einstein.
>
> 'And after that?', the mother asked again.
>
> 'Even more fairy tales', answered Einstein, waving his pipe.
>
> (Lindø 1988, p. 11)

We must train ourselves to see what is not there, as the lamb story above makes clear. That's creativity, right there. And what's the impulse behind it? The child brought the sheep back to life because she was attached to it, the companion she had come to know over the year since it was a little lamb. She felt duty-bound to lift it up and give it warmth; the frozen joint was so cold where it lay on the worktop. And what a fine job she did.

So what exactly is this ability to form inner pictures, this capacity for imagination? In his book *Words in Place*, Paul Matthews (2007, p. 36) compiles a list of answers that pupils from his creative writing class at Emerson College have given to that question:

> Imagination is seeing pictures the world's heart has wished for.
> Imagination is the ability to be part of the Creation as the creator.
> It is breathing into things, entering into an inner dialogue with the world.
> To be imaginative is to be present in the presence of things.

Imagination is breathing and rhythm as you enter into an inner dialogue with things themselves – and are present in their presence – or it is throwing your heart over the stream and trusting your body to follow. It's at once acrobatics and magic, internal and completely invisible. It's the ability to be partner and co-creator in the creative weave of life. With imagination's help the creative human being can 'see with the heart' and know what the world, or the other, needs and longs for. Empathy springs from imagination. As do words and language, says Zarathustra: 'The ability to form images (imagination and fantasy) … reaches highest. Words, pictures, and language gradually emerge from it, multiply by it.' (Surti 1981, p. 35)

Developing the capacity for imagination is partly a process of self-creation, finding your values and individuality and making use of your personal resources. On the other hand, it involves finding your feet in the world, locating where you want to plant your ideas and values, making space and identifying your location's distinctive potential. As partners on earth with all evolving life, we look for a place where we can develop ourselves. This requires us to dare to form attachments and engage in dialogue, interaction and activity with others. To pull this off, we need the interpersonal skills of the Ash Lad.

Venturing the unknown

The Norwegian folk hero the Ash Lad goes by many names but is not good for much except blowing the embers in the fireplace. He is often looked down upon, and yet he's open, trusting, helpful and helped. The Ash Lad achieves magical things, solves the problems he meets on his way and makes his dreams come true. He creates freedom and new perspective (Sundland 1995, p. 33).

When the fire dies out on the hearth something fateful occurs. Old and safe values lose their ability to give life meaning. The Ash Lad stands for new hope, creativity, knowledge and energy. His approach to the world is original, playful and imaginative; he is the original artist. He is creative where his elder brothers are ineffectual. The Ash Lad sees more in all things; the real is behind all appearances.

His brothers, Per and Paul, do not see through their own eyes but through the eyes of others. As a result they always fall flat. The Ash Lad's mission is to create new values to replace those which are lost. These do not come free; he must struggle for them. He must win the new values himself. His way of doing things is to connect with others. The Ash Lad wants freedom with all the risks that it entails; spontaneity rather than control over his surroundings. He dares to go it alone and defy convention. His adventures paint a world full of wonder, where under the surface life pulses, waiting to be released (Sundland 1995, p. 39).

The princess who always had to have the last word

There was once a king who had a daughter who was so wayward and wilful in her speech that she always had to have the last word. Therefore he promised that he who could make her hold her tongue should get the Princess and half the kingdom into the bargain.

There were plenty who wanted to try, you may believe it, for it's not every day that you can get a king's daughter and half a kingdom. The gate to the King's manor didn't stop swinging for a moment; they came in flocks and droves, from east and west, both riding and walking. But there was no one who could make the Princess stop talking. At last the King made it known that those who tried but failed would be branded on both ears with that big branding iron of his. He wouldn't have all these people running to his manor for nothing.

Now there were three brothers who had heard tell of the Princess, and, as they weren't well off where they lived, they wanted to go and try their luck and see if they could win the King's daughter and half the kingdom. They got along pretty well with each other, and so they went together, all three.

When they had gone a bit of the way, the youngest brother, who was called the Ash Lad, found a dead magpie. 'Look what I found!', he shouted.

'What've you found?' asked his brothers.

'I found a dead magpie', he said.

'Fie! Drop it! What are you going to do with that?', said the two, who always thought they were the wisest.

'Oh, I've nothing better to do, and nothing better to carry, so I'll just take it along with me', said the Ash Lad.

When they had gone a bit farther, the Ash Lad found an old willow ringlet. 'Look what I found! Look what I found!', he shouted.

'What've you found now?', said his brothers.

'I found a willow hank', he replied.

'Pooh! What are you going to do with that? Drop it!', said the two.

'I've nothing better to do, and nothing better to carry, so I'll just take it along with me', said the Ash Lad.

When they had gone a little farther, he found a bit of a broken saucer. 'Boys! Look what I found! Look what I found!'

'Well, what did you find now?', asked the brothers.

'A bit of broken saucer', he said.

'Ugh! Now that was something to take along! Drop it!', they said.

'Oh, I've nothing better to do, and nothing better to carry, so I'll just take it along with me', replied the Ash Lad.

When they had gone a little farther, he found a crooked ram's horn and just after that he found the mate to it. 'Look what I found! Look what I found, boys!', he shouted. 'What've you found now?'

'Two ram's horns', replied the Ash Lad.

'Ugh, drop them! What are you going to do with them?'

'Oh, I've nothing better to do, and nothing better to carry, so I'll just take them along with me', said the Ash Lad.

In a little while he found a wedge. 'But, fellas, look what I found! Look what I found!', he shouted.

'That's a mighty lot of finding you've been doing! What have you found this time?', said the two eldest.

'I found a wedge', he replied.

'Oh, drop it! What are you going to do with that?'

'I've nothing better to do, and nothing better to carry, so I'll just take it along with me', said the Ash Lad.

As they walked over the fields near the King's manor – where manure had recently been spread – the Ash Lad bent down and picked up a worn-out shoe sole. 'Say, fellas! Look what I found! Look what I found!'

'If only you'd find a little sense by the time you got there!', said the two. 'What did you find this time?'

'A worm-out shoe sole.'

'Ugh! That was really something to pick up! Drop it! What are you going to do with it?'

'Oh, I've nothing better to do, and nothing better to carry, so I'll just take it along so I can win the Princess and half the kingdom', said the Ash Lad.

'Yes, you're likely to do that, you are!', said the two.

And then they arrived and were let in to see the Princess. First, the eldest.

'Good day', he said.

'Good day yourself', she said, twisting and turning.

'It's terrible warm in here', he said.

'It's warmer in the coals', replied the Princess.

There lay the branding iron, ready and waiting. When he saw this, his courage failed him right away, and so it was all up with him.

The middle brother didn't fare any better.

'Good day', he said.

'Good day yourself', she said, starting to squirm.

'It's terrible hot in here', he said.

'It's hotter in the coals', she said.

At that, he too lost both voice and speech, and so it was out with the iron again.

Then came the Ash Lad.

'Good day', he said.

'Good day, yourself', she replied, twisting and turning.

'It's good and warm in here', said the Ash Lad.

'It's warmer in the coals', she replied. A third one didn't make her temper any sweeter.

'I suppose I can roast my magpie there, then?', he asked.

'I'm afraid she'll burst', said the King's daughter.

'Oh, that be no trouble. I'll put this willow hank around it', replied the boy.

'It's too wide!', she said.

'I'll drive in a wedge', said the boy, and took out the wedge.

'All the fat'll run off her!', said the King's daughter.

'I'll catch it in this', replied the boy, and he held up the bit of broken saucer.

'You're twisting my words!', said the Princess.

'No! Your words aren't twisted, but this is', replied the boy, and he took out one of the ram's horns.

'Well! I've never seen the like!', shouted the Princess.

'Here's the like of it', said the boy, and he took out the other one.

'You're bent on wearing me out, aren't you?', she said.

'No, you're not worn out, but this is!', replied the boy, and he pulled out the shoe sole.

The Princess was speechless. 'Now, you're mine!', said the Ash Lad, and so he got her, and half the kingdom into the bargain.

Theodor Kittelsen has interpreted this motif of the Ash Lad (Figure 5.1). Do you see the lad wondering? What drives him? Who or what is he in dialogue with? You see him from behind; he is looking into the horizon. Is this golden castle something he sees outside or inside himself? Is he dreaming about it or picturing it? We can tell he's already wandered far in difficult terrain to reach this point; finally, after much striving, his vision or picture is clear to him! Nor will the rest of his journey be easy. He must descend into the valley again and likely lose sight of the castle (his vision). It's uncertain whether he will find it again – but whatever happens he needs to trust that he will find his way. He cannot give up. He must venture into the unknown, get his bearings there, cultivate this space for inner growth and connect to himself and others. Perhaps the way is itself the goal.

Figure 5.1. The Ashladd and the Soria Moria Castel by Theodor Kittelsen.

FOR REFLECTION:
What is your 'Soria Moria Castle' or inner image and longing? What does it look like? Can you put it into words, lines or colours? Or perhaps a sound, song or tones?

The character and growth of place

> Education shall foster both loyalty towards our heritage and an urge to break new ground. Hence it must provide both practical skills and insight, training of both head and hand. (NCC 1997, p. 5)

When the Nærøyfjord was put on the UNESCO world heritage list in 2005, the reason was geological. In few other places in the world can we see geological processes so visibly altering and recreating the basis for life. In winter, frosts cause masses of rock, soil and ice to tumble in great landslides. In summer, water rushes down the mountain sides as streams hunt out new routes and cut new channels in the loose material. Stories of the elements ruling and recreating nature are a regular feature of the Norse myths and sagas. So the landscape is undergoing a continual process of creation that we can see happening before our very eyes. Listen to the beginning of the Norse creation myth from Snorri's *Edda*, where the whole world is created in the meeting *between* the elements:

> In the beginning there were only two realms: to the south lay the home of heat, fire, embers and the blinding light, this realm was called Muspelheim; to the north lay the home of frost, cold, rain, fog and ice, this realm was called Nivlheim. Between the two realms was a great, gaping black chasm called Ginnungagapet. One day, cold air blew from the north and mixed with the warm air from the south. It started to drip, and from this dripping life emerged … and life took the form of a giant. His name was Ymir. (Sturluson 2005)

In this Norse epic we glimpse a belief or attitude to life that was formed in the struggle between opposites, between north and south, ice and fire. Creative power arises from a tension between opposites in the same way as a child is created by the tension between man and woman (Birgisson 2013, p. 73). Education too has a number of seemingly contradictory aims to balance. For example, the Norwegian curriculum says, 'We must open the senses to the patterns that have taken hold as traditions, in everything from music to architecture – and have the courage to think anew and the imagination to break with established ways' (NCC 1997, p. 21).

Interaction and cultural history

> You must give birth to your images. They are the future waiting to be born. (Rainer Maria Rilke quoted in Gersie et al. 2014, p. 317)

Many tales in Indre Sogn tell about the close ties people once had to nature. They reveal how dependent people were on one another, for better or worse. Because it was so vital to be on good terms with each other, they had to consciously nurture fellowship among themselves. Over the generations, people had learnt to cooperate with neighbours and the elements to survive. Most of the mountain farms were worked until 1900. One story tells of a man called Knut in the Aurland Valley who was so bothered by a wood nymph that he packed his trunk and emigrated to America; the elemental forces were getting too strident in the valley. When his ship sailed from the fjord, people observed a woman standing on the quay, weeping. No one knew her; they kept their thoughts to themselves. The old ways of farming were waning.

Some of our local stories are recorded in archives, but a significant part of them is written in rock and soil. In the valley large heaps of stones tell of field clearances and cultivation. Long walls and ditches are still visible; barns, outbuildings, barrows and sacred stones are overgrown with scrub. How can these cultural treasures be rediscovered and given new substance? How to carry the past into the future?

Our mission today is to act with respect for the special characteristics of a place and to develop it further through creative activities. Does the place have any specific needs or purpose? What values does it hold? Is it possible to allow the place itself to have a say, via its particular character or atmosphere? Are we using our ability to be present also to hear our surroundings and enter into dialogue with them? Creative work requires changing tack and broadening perspectives. It means developing the ability to comprehend and take care of things that are outside oneself – things that can motivate us beyond narrow self-interest. Karin Sveen writes in the poem 'Blessed Are the Poor in Spirit',

> Make me poor in spirit.
> Drain it as a pot of my Self and fill it with other water.
> Let me be fulfilled and overflow; my thoughts will follow like a little boat. (Nyhus 2009, p. 92)

In order to know something about the world or a place, we need to stand apart as well as take part in it. We must practise seeing the place and ourselves from without and from within; we must learn to shift focus and point of view. Do the visual arts have anything to tell us here?

Practising new ways of seeing

> [A] confrontation with creative art can wrench us out of our habitual modes of thought, challenge our opinions, and provide experiences that spur us to re-examine prevailing conceptions and break with conventional wisdom and customary modes. (NCC 1997, p. 6)

In his book *Nattlandene* [Nightlands], Christian Norberg-Schulz describes the North as a mood-world of restless forces. He singles out landscape painting's ability to communicate something of this play of forces and nocturnal atmosphere. To make us recognize something we didn't realize we knew, all art forms make the known unknown. The poetic mode frees our gaze and opens us to new insights. To discover the art in art is to acknowledge the possibility of alternative parallel worlds. Art creates strangeness in order to bring the familiar into relief. In the strange we see the general and the commonplace.

Nikolai Astrup paints his native landscape as he experienced it in childhood. He paints as though the land were hidden in the memory of a lost time – a time when the world was whole, before doubt, questions and difficult choices came. He recreates an inner experience of a lost paradise. This gives us a deeper sense of place – not just of his childhood home, but of what any place is, of *the existing* of places. In his painting is something universal that people are looking for. He takes us to the core of his experience of nature, as in *Spring Night in the Garden* (see p. 112). Astrup rebuilds, as it were, his poetic worlds from within – and sense creates the world he depicts.

Such universal experiences as those Astrup explored while painting familiar scenes in the Western Norwegian setting were dear to his heart. He went home to find himself, and through what was close and personal to him he touched the universal (Loge 2005, p. 196).

Vinjum went away in order to understand the mountains and the Sognefjord. Perhaps it's impossible to grasp the value in ourselves before we have understood and appreciated the foreign or the unknown. Only when we have grasped the universal within us can we see how valuable it is – so valuable that we want to pass it on to others. When confronted with the unknown or the foreign we ask ourselves: Who are we? What do we have to offer? We like to share, after all; to see what we have in the cupboard that we can bring to the party.

> Education should elaborate and deepen the learners' familiarity with national and local traditions – the domestic history and distinctive features that are our contribution to cultural diversity in the world. (NCC 1997, p. 4)

Living thinking

> Education shall not only transmit learning; it shall also provide learners with the ability to acquire and attain new knowledge themselves. The aim of education is to train pupils in both synthesis and analysis – to develop both imagination and scepticism so that experience can be translated into insight. Scientific method develops both the creative and critical senses. (NCC 1997, p. 7)

For dead thinking, understanding the idea is enough. Dead thinking reproduces thoughts and ideas, whereas living thinking seeks to generate them. This means that one cannot simply copy someone else's idea or model; one has to understand and expand on the underlying thinking and work creatively from one's own viewpoint. You cannot simply copy and paste ideas. They need be grounded in experience. Olav H. Hauge writes in the poem 'Don't Come to Me with the Entire Truth',

> Don't come to me with the entire truth.
> Don't bring the ocean if I feel thirsty,
> nor heaven if I ask for light;
> but bring a hint, some dew, a particle,
> as birds carry drops away from a lake,
> and the wind a grain of salt.
> (Bly and Hedin 2008, p. 13)

Is it not in the tensions between heat and cold, between creative and critical faculties, that something new can arise? At times, one has to leave the familiar and the comfortable behind, work across disciplines, venture into the unknown and form new relationships. In school, pupils must become aware of the limitations of predominant ways of thinking and realize that established doctrines can block fresh insight. An example is the divide between arts and sciences. Can we reconsider the notion that artists and researchers must live in separate worlds? Do researchers have sole access to 'the truth', and artists a monopoly on creativity? Is there a middle way, where values and ethics can have a say?

For reflection:

What does it mean for you as a teacher to work creatively? How can you make space for creative elements in your subject at your school?

CHAPTER SIX

WORKING

To understand the transformation in play in human growth and development, we need to glimpse the inherent, languageless dialogue that we enter through engaging with our environment through our senses, actions and being. This dialogue starts small, when an infant first makes eye contact and simply is in this togetherness with the parent. A little circle is drawn within the universe. And inside it, although as yet without words, a bond is formed that is a space for transformation. Now the infant can learn to imitate, and we adults can be rejuvenated by the encounter – which is a dialogue, a reciprocal exchange. Becoming is not something that has to be inserted into this form of togetherness, because to be in this connection of looks, gestures and, eventually, words is to be *in* transformation. Here we see that language originates in what we may call wordless dialogue.

Work's inner and outer sides

We never lose this faculty for understanding by wordlessly sharing the other's smile or laughter, sadness or tears. But we develop new forms of language which we gradually learn to master like free-standing tools we can use to express ourselves with: spoken language, written language, music and dance, painting and drawing, and so on. All these forms of language allow you to give expression to your existence, to make your inner life visible.

> Work is not merely a means of earning a livelihood. It is intrinsic to the human personality to test, express and extend skills through work. (NCC 1997, p. 8)

Looking at the whole range of expressive and creative capability, we see that all crafts and all technology may similarly be considered extensions of human expression. In other words, our identity grows in two directions rather like a tree does. It grows down and into the world through our senses and participation in the world – and it grows up and out by the means we acquire to express ourselves, with new branches for each form of language and on each branch new fruits we can give the world. When addressing questions of language development, schools need to appreciate the relationship between inner and outer dimensions: our connecting to the world with body and senses (roots) nourishes the linguistic expression in speech and writing that is able to develop (branches, fruit).

Creating spaces where learning can happen

It takes time to organize things before twenty 15–16-year-olds can come for practical farming experience at the agricultural college. Both colleagues and pupils need to be ready. It's important to prepare the ground for your project so that the pupils feel well received. This is a sensitive issue at their age. Do others care about me? Am I welcome? Colleagues should be informed in good time and their preparations well supported. Along the way, one must be able to interpret the possibilities of the place and know how to use them creatively.

> Knowledge in action exists in the doing, not in any underlying theory, and it can be acquired by practice, but not learnt in the form of theory. (Molander 1993, p. 136)

If we are going to be outdoors, we have to be prepared for all weathers. We must keep moving, ready to change our minds, to be open to what comes our way. Just because the goals are clear does not make the path and the journey any less important. It is a dynamic exchange between goal and process which ties it all together, an interactional skill in which transformative learning *can* emerge but is never guaranteed. Here are two examples of how to create space for teaching that puts pupils at the centre.

There is a need today to somehow give teaching back to young people and start from where they are standing. If we can manage to introduce a task or project in a way that touches their will and feelings, then we are well on our way. If pupils take ownership of the process they are going to engage in, they will be self-motivated. Preparation in the form of anchoring and igniting interest is a condition for getting started. This phase often takes longer than you might think, but it's worth it, as you'll see later in the process. Once the pupils have identified with the task and understand their role in it, we are off and running.

The art of baking

In the village we have several small-scale enterprises, one of which is a bakery cafe that offers locally sourced food. Marianne's Bakery and Cafe is a meeting place that enlivens the senses.

Marianne's baking invites us in and you might say she kneads the local community into her dough; she drives community change with her bakery. She knows the art of baking: it's as though through her bread we can taste and be nourished by her values. She believes in her work. She makes her dough with care and mindfulness, using organic flour from local grains, little yeast and long raising times. The slow process makes the bread moist and flavoursome.

Bakers need critical sense and discretion – being good with their hands is not enough. They have to know how many loaves they can sell, maintain quality standards and offer an atmosphere and setting that customers will want to return to. On top of this, Marianne also wants to develop her business as a learning arena for youth work training.

Café founder Marianne, holding bread, with her good helpers. Photograph: Jorunn Barane

Important social skills can be practised here in interactions with customers. The trainees get instant feedback about the products they serve and can feel they are actively contributing to the community.

Making flatbread

First up on today's schedule is flatbread making, and joining me are six big 16-year-olds, all of them boys. Before entering the smokehouse with the dough under my arm, I think to myself: Why am I doing this? What can baking flatbread possibly have to do with 16-year-olds? It's so old-fashioned. Isn't it time to think of something else?

The room is ready with baking board, hotplates and the flat sticks we use to lift the rolled-out dough rounds from the board to the hotplate. The boys fill the room, happy to be indoors today. The fire crackles in the wood oven. The place smells of smoke and burnt flour exactly as a bakehouse should. We seat ourselves around the baking board and I start to talk: about the grain which is grown on the farm and ground at the mill, about the milk which we ferment and strain, how the whey was used in the dough and how the curd becomes cheese. Everything is ethically and organically produced on the farm. The boys listen closely. Now it is time to knead the dough to the right consistency. Next comes the rolling out, a technique that requires long practice.

> 'Patrick' is a fine lad, tall and dark-haired, but he sits in a slouch and his gaze is glassy and inward. It is difficult to reach him. It's as though nothing matters to him. But, no, he lets out a sigh. After many attempts he can finally roll out rounds, dip them in sesame seeds and bake them – he's lightening up now. The rhythm of the group is slow; they need a break before having another go. But they work steadily if I keep their spirits up, even when the thin rounds break in two. And their conversation is flowing, a world I'm not part of; it is *their* session. Now it's time to add herbs, garlic and salt to the curd cheese. Patrick is sent out to the garden to find what he needs, then he makes the cheese and seems astonished by the fact that it works. We reward ourselves with a taste. Patrick spreads cheese on a freshly baked flatbread. Suddenly he jumps up, whacks the table with his rolling pin and exclaims, 'That was bloody delicious!' He runs to tell the others. He is eating and somehow can't get enough.

Something happened to Patrick that day; it was as though he attached himself to the world. Through his senses he made a connection between his inner self and the outer work. He broke new ground. It was as though he mobilized himself and the whole place in a new way. For the remainder of the week he worked independently and on his own initiative.

On being present in the here and now

The essence here is to start from the pupils' experience as participants in the world. This is not simply a question of external knowledge; it is about fostering human growth and connecting knowledge to life. Hence the importance of 'doing things' and grasping things in one's hands. A variety of tasks can be useful here. Although baking flatbread may seem old-fashioned, it works wonders for young people. We have tested it often and we are just as amazed every time. Past and future are immaterial; what matters is being present with the youngsters in the here and now, finding peace and rhythm, moving, performing a task, using your hands and being in the moment. For young people it is about being touched in some way through their senses and emotions. Then they are able to connect more deeply both to themselves and to others. From this perspective, there are any number of 'old-fashioned' tasks on a farm which can serve this purpose – hay drying, cheese-making, wood chopping, horse packing, etc. – tasks in which the aesthetic and ethical dimensions reside in the activity itself, through the work task, the social context and the interaction between participants. Just as with learning goals in conventional school subjects, it is important that learners practise personal qualities that are transferable to other situations. Key qualities of this kind include creativity, the ability to improvise, initiative, curiosity, the abilities to take in interest in things and to learn.

Living as we do in a fragmented world makes it harder to connect the dots and see things in context. One of the most important ways teachers can help is by creating learning situations in which this ability is encouraged. For young people this means being allowed to come closer to themselves, to be in the here and now. Given this opportunity, they will connect to themselves and to nature. Too often our professional skills and motivations as teachers get in the way.

Learning and teamwork in making apple juice

The press, strainer, cloth, buckets and tubs are ready. I know from experience that this is a good learning arena. The work is concrete and the tasks are straightforward. It demands good teamwork, precision, cleanliness, manual dexterity, rhythm and a sense of overview.

Yesterday the pupils gathered apples, learnt about sorting, classification, the different varieties, how to handle the fruit, etc. Early this morning the first group of seven 16-year-olds arrived. They are tired. Some of them plonk themselves down and one girl, 'Ida', begins to complain loudly. Irritated, I snap something back at her. It comes out of nowhere, but to my surprise I see it waking something in her, a spark that we could really use right now. Then I run through the procedure, explain how the grinder works, things to watch out for, the actual pressing, and the pasteurization at the end.

Now they are looking for things to do, eager to get started. Ida, in particular, is making an effort. She gets to her feet, takes charge and allocates tasks to the others in the group. I step back to let them find their own rhythm. I listen, make small adjustments, ever present and attentive; although it is their session you have to be ready to help them along if they trip up, and to establish a nonverbal connection to guide them. It's about becoming a team and finding their purpose in fellowship, of trying things out, learning skills, experiencing, and using their senses.

They cheer when the juice starts to run down into the bucket. The juice tastes incredibly fresh; it is the pupils' accomplishment and they can feel rightly proud. Ida has led the group with a steady hand today. At the end she stands there, hands firmly on hips, and declares her ambition to be an apple farmer by the fjord. This is something she can master – 'So just wait, you'll see'. From her demeanour and words, it is plain she has broken new ground. She has found a new way to lead, in both herself and her setting. For the rest of that week, she worked independently.

Reflection from the class

The secondary school pupils who came for farm experience told us that their stay brought home to them just how much food means in our lives. One pupil learnt to appreciate the effort that goes into a farm; there was much more to land work than he had expected. A number of pupils said that as a result of the week their working stamina and patience had improved. All of them had newfound respect for farmers and their work. Many said they had forged new friendships in their class and got on better with their classmates. Some remarked that their self-confidence had improved. One boy with long arms and cumbersome movements said he felt better in himself, and perhaps a little lighter. Yes, it takes time and practice to put into words what is happening inwardly.

Place as an arena for transformative learning

> Human identity presupposes place identity. For life to take place, place must be understood and respected. This is forgotten today, and the result is loss of place and a connected crisis of identity. (Norberg-Schulz 1993)

How does place itself influence the learning process and the *capacity to change* or the transformative power that arises in a learning situation? This is a central question that we shall explore a little further here. From Patrick's revelation while baking flatbread and Ida's transformative experience of apple pressing, we see that both pupils felt at one with the place, with the bakehouse or the farmyard. Their experiences were embedded in a community atmosphere of work, similar to what used to happen in this space. They succeeded where other competent people had succeeded before them! This self-awareness is an important *impulse* that often manifests either as a strong physical sensation or in a vivid inner vision. The boy was impelled to run to fetch the others; the girl could see herself as a fruit farmer by the fjord.

Motivation lies behind our actions, but where does it come from and what role do the relationships between learner and environment play? What do we mean when we say that we are motivated? If we are motivated, do we feel like doing something? Are we willing, or have we decided, to do something? Motivation can be an intention, in which case we are focused on doing something; but just as easily a situation may arise that demands specific action – we might have to make an effort (resistance) to carry out the apple pressing in a group. Once we make it through our resistance and find our creative power, it is possible that afterwards, like Patrick with his flatbread, we will have the impetus to tackle new work tasks. He worked independently the rest of the week. Illeris believes (2013, p. 148) that it is necessary to consider both the internal motivation in the form of desire, interest, engagement, conviction, and the external motivation in the form of demands, necessity, or in some cases compulsion. Further, he notes, it can often be understood that internal motivation is *better* or *stronger* or *more genuine* than external motivation. This depends on the situation and is a complicated matter. What matters is how these different kinds of motivation interact. When it comes to transformative learning, motivation is central. People don't change (identity, behaviour, etc.) if there is not a strong motivation to do so. Transformative learning is always a condition with important emotional and social dimensions (ibid., p. 156).

School is an integral part of local community

> School is not a waystation in life, but a society in miniature. (NCC 1997, p. 30)

If we take a look around us, we see buildings and objects with histories. People have made and shaped what surrounds us – even a non-descript concrete wall has been designed and built by someone. The feeling of being able to shape our surroundings and express ourselves through them is one of the most essential conditions for feeling at home in a place.

What difference does it make if we have plants in the classroom? They don't just have botanical value. They make us feel at home partly because they are there creating an atmosphere of life, partly because we have a duty to take care of them. These two reasons together contribute to our sense of place. When it comes to childhood and growing up, it is essential that children experience that they really can shape their surroundings – including the school grounds where they spend many years of their lives. We learn 'to care' by caring.

The school garden at ABU represents the innermost circle in the Aurland model. It has been in use since 1994. During Classes 1–6, each class has a plot to cultivate which they link to the subject of food and health. The health researcher Antonovsky (1987) claims there are three fundamental prerequisites for a person to feel a sense of connection (*coherence*) in life. The world must be perceived as *comprehensible*, so that things seem clear and intelligible. The world must feel *meaningful*, so that you feel at home in it. The world must also be *manageable*, that is, you can step in and make a difference. After many years of cultivation, it was time to give the garden a boost. The course 'The Farm as a Pedagogical Resource' was an opportunity for professional development and to discuss the next steps for the garden and Living School (see Chapter 3). One of the resulting projects was to raise starter plants in the greenhouse and sell the surplus vegetable plants and herbs on the square in Vangen. The Class 5 entrepreneurship project 'From Seed to Plant' now runs annually and is integrated into the school's plans.

Entrepreneurship in Class 5: from seed to plant

The project's learning objectives are divided into three according to the 'connective model for didactic design' of Hiim and Hippe (2001, p. 30). In terms of *attitudes* the goal is: 'appreciation of food and consideration for what grows, locally produced food and the path from seed to table, ecological recycling agriculture and sustainable development'. Then come the goals of *knowledge* in botany, and *skills* in: cultivation according to organic principles, manual dexterity, and collaboration and shared responsibility for taking care of the seedlings.

The work demands responsibility, precision and teamwork, but it's worth all that when spring arrives and the plants are healthy, plump and green. Getting ready for market, collecting plants and tables, making posters, doing publicity and inviting friends and relatives to the spring sale are both fun and challenging. When pupils meet customers who see the process behind the product and share their thoughts, they are really and truly part of the community. They are proud, of course. Their plants are of the best quality and they've grown them themselves – where else could you get hold of such fine specimens? Moreover, the pupils know the plants' names and can advise customers on how they develop and what nutrients they need. 'This is the best day of my life', said one of the girls. She had invited all her relatives to visit the stall.

In this moment the pupils realize that they can contribute to, and are a part of, society. Their experience tells them it is possible to step in and make a difference. They are needed. 'Good teaching will give pupils evidence of succeeding in their work, faith in their own abilities, and the heart to take responsibility for their own learning and their own lives' (NCC 1997, p. 19).

Market stall. Photograph: ABU

According to the eco-philosopher Sigmund K. Setreng (2014, p. 126), the key to moving towards an ecologically centred society is to be found in 'meaningful work'. Meaningful work, as he defines it, fulfils the following five criteria:

1. It is activity necessary for material survival.
2. Through practical activity the diversity of individual potential is brought into bloom, and along with it the unfolding and maturation of personality.
3. Its challenges prompt the individual's loyalty to the group and capacity for cooperation to develop.
4. Its products (goods and services) enhance and strengthen life in society and nature – they do not break down, damage or pollute.
5. It engages children – not just in play, but in a way that both they and adults regard as socially useful.

Setreng underlines the importance of the fifth point, because here work is handed back to the community as the primary basis for bringing up children. He concludes with an appeal to include children before all else (ibid., p. 127).

For reflection:
How can you develop meaningful work at your school? How can you contribute to social sustainability in your school and community?

CHAPTER SEVEN

KNOWLEDGE

> A good all-round general education includes concrete knowledge about the human being, society and nature which can provide a broad outlook and perspective; know-how and maturity to face life's practical, social and personal challenges; qualities and values that facilitate cooperation between people and make it enriching and exciting for them to live together. (NCC 1997, p. 13)

What about reading and writing? What about arithmetic? And general knowledge? Do the pupils learn enough? This is where everything gets turned on its head. Because it's nice, now, to sit in the classroom after being out in the landscape. Before we went outside, we read a text. Now, at our leisure, we can write and draw about our experiences. The room falls silent when the exercise starts: we are going to recollect our experiences, see the whole picture in our memory, let our thoughts retrieve it, hold on to it, judge it, find words to give it expression, combine the words into short sentences. The teacher goes around the room. The class has a certain peace about it, a calm that comes with writing.

What carries us over from experiences to general education is the release of thinking from the hands, from the experience in which it first emerged. For this to happen, learning needs to alternate between experience and reflection. The processing of experience, the drawing and writing afterwards, is done with care. The two areas are mutually reinforcing. If the experience of a topic is memorable, then the writing and reflection about it will be fuller, more nuanced and precise – also, the act of writing will be more fun, and pupils' time to exercise their thoughts and ideas following the experience will stand them in good stead when next they encounter comparable areas of experience and activity. In this way, a synergy can evolve between nurturing our capacities for work and for knowledge. The bedrock of all-round education is thus a rich experiential life. By having experiences, learners acquire the ability to see and understand connections, to gain an overview and to look at things from different perspectives.

A number of schools are now starting to 'flip the classroom'. The increasingly popular 'flipped classroom' model uses lesson time not to feed pupils with concepts but to process them. This is a radical innovation. The vehicle for this reversal of traditional classroom teaching is information technology. Instead of using homework to review and reinforce what the teacher has presented in class, pupils learn the material via online videos they can access on their own devices. As a result, time at school is freed for processing, conversation and reflection. Transforming the classroom from a lecture theatre to a space for reflection, conversation and personal expression is the key to developing general education in schools in the future.

Practising multiple ways of thinking

We often assume that thinking is poles apart from creativity. Thought is clear; it sheds light on things and also helps us to take a detached view, to analyse and assess. Thought is as diverse as the questions we ask. So, for instance, building a den, a cabin, a bird house or a windmill requires thinking. When we turn to the practicalities of a task, we invariably find that there is more than one way to go about it: different ways to design things, different sequences of steps to chose from. If we are experienced in a particular field, the thinking that accompanies our actions is flexible and creative. It finds new solutions, good solutions. It experiments, encounters failure, works out a better way, then another one – until it suddenly finds a way to solve a problem which surpasses our previous method. The same is true of finding good forms of working together. Here, too, are challenges with more than one possible solution. They are dynamic as well, meaning that their solutions must constantly be created anew. All work of a practical and social nature, in other words, needs an awareness that is questioning, observant and investigative. As we described in the barrow-clearing example in Chapter 3, the group figures out both its working method and effective ways of collaborating. This requires thought. And when thinking is in the mode of not yet knowing, when it is investigative, then it is transformative. After deliberating and putting ideas to the test, we may find ourselves in a different place than before. Something is transformed, because all understanding changes the understander.

> By creative talent we mean the ability to find new solutions to practical problems by untried moves and unused methods. (NCC 1997, p. 5)

If our future is to be sustainable, we must envision what is possible and will help to enable transformation. By asking the right questions and considering the underlying values that guide our choices, we can eventually find a way there. The next example illustrates how cultural heritage not only relates to the past, but is a creative process in which school plays a vital part.

From earth to grain to bread

This is a project for Class 9 about the sowing, harvesting and grinding of grain. The knowledge goals are: locally produced food; preparing the soil for sowing; sowing and grinding the grain; different types of grain; nutritional value; crop rotation; and organic farming principles.

The skills goals: the ability to turn earth with spade, rake and harrow; the ability to sow evenly with a sowing fiddle and cover the grain; concentration, patience, initiative, perseverance, cooperation.

The attitudinal goals: awareness of oneself; holistic thinking; seeing connections in nature which we are part of; acting locally, thinking globally; local food, identity and belonging; developing local hospitableness and community awareness.

> Pupils should be able to explain relationships between natural resources, business, their living environment and way of life. (Utdanningsdirektoratet 2006)

To grind the grain, the pupils visit Evald Knutsen, a pensioner in Flåm. They want to do it the old way and Evald has reconstructed a traditional flour mill on his farm. Our goal is to show how water can be used to do work. Evald describes how his mill came to be, from cutting and laying the timbers, and making the 'old miller' (the water wheel), all the way to the finished millhouse. He also explains the grain hopper, the millstone and the frame surrounding it. This is our cultural heritage, he points out. We pour the grain, barley, into the hopper. Then the whole group goes to open the sluice and watch as the water courses down to the wheel, which starts to turn and drive the millstone. We ground 5.3 kg of flour that day.

The pupils have sowed barley on the school farm, then reaped, dried, threshed and now ground it into flour. Afterwards they bake bread. In order to thank Evald and to serve him what they have made from the flour, they invite him to Easter breakfast. They have followed the whole process from seed to bread, and in doing so gained insight into the origins of food, grain and flour. In Figure 7.1 we see how proud Evald is. His knowledge is still useful.

Class 9 serve breakfast with bread made from grain they have grown themselves and ground at Evald's mill (he looks pleased). Photograph: Cecilie Bugge.

Developing the ability to see connections

In the grain-to-bread example above, the object is not so much to develop skills as to give pupils the chance to identify and understand connections. Understanding a process comprising several stages, each with its own distinct requirements, is not as easy as one-two-three. It takes time to comprehend something that itself takes time. The pedagogical approach taken here is to address each stage individually and understand it fully. Then, having passed through the stages concretely, the learner can look back on the journey and see an arc, a connection – consisting, within each of its stages, of still more connections. In in education that emphasizes the context of what is being experienced, pupils get systematic practice in spotting connections and so develop their capacity for synthetic thought. There's no need for them to theorize their way to the whole picture; rather it comes to them through taking part in the journey. This is sustainable all-round general education because it nurtures thinking that is free and independent yet takes into consideration the connections that hold life together.

The material is the teacher

As a mentor, one has to discover for oneself the knowledge tacit in a process, then set up experiential learning situations that can be adapted to the individual. To achieve a desired outcome, a practised craftsman often seems to perform actions automatically. What is their secret? In the box below are the words of a glassblower in reply to the question, 'What do you learn from blowing glass?'

> I have to understand the materiality of glass, the fluidity and heat in the process: that's where the motivation and inspiration are. You must believe in yourself, have self-confidence and humility. You mustn't give up. It's trial and error over and over. You need to be patient. What I find important and inspiring is having to team up with the material, the glass. There's a lot of coordination involved. My hands are doing different things but working together. Everything has to work together; it's a challenge because it all has to happen so quickly. I have to stay on my toes and be present in my mind and body. I also have to think lightning fast; pausing for thought is out of the question. The challenge is thinking quickly enough and engaging your thoughts instantly. It takes lots and lots of practice. You need physical strength and a good memory. You know you are improving when your results improve. You must understand and cooperate with glass as fluid material, and be humble about it. Also, don't take yourself too seriously. You need to cope with coming up short, with the realization that it could have been better. I learn how to communicate and cooperate.

It is in the encounter with matter itself that learning takes place; it is the fluid, hot glass that forms the glassblower. When you are deeply absorbed in an activity, it is the material that offers resistance. This resistance, which contact with all material brings, is the very essence of self-regulated learning. An ostensibly simple thing like holding a tool and using it correctly – a spade, for example – can only be learnt through practice, not instantly mastered. When we are involved in a task and the resistance it affords, self-adjustment and balancing naturally begin in everything we do, physically as well as mentally. Parallel to this adjustment, skills are formed with which we might handle anything. In his theory of salutogenesis, Antonovsky (Eriksson and Lindström 2006) defines this ability to take care of things, or rather the skills necessary to learn to do so, as 'manageability' – and says it is one of the three fundamental components of 'human health'. Such qualities can only be developed through resistance. The challenge for schools is to provide the optimal type of resistance. Just as Vygotsky talks of a zone of proximal development with respect to cognitive and intellectual challenges, so there is a corresponding zone in creative work. In craftwork the hands do the experiencing and make adjustments, as a result of which self-regulating process the pupil gradually acquires skill.

From their own experience, mentor teachers can map what resistance and processes lie hidden in different craft areas, and prepare development paths adapted to the emotional, physical and cognitive needs of each individual pupil. This brings us to the topic of place- and craft-based special education.

Special education

During the transition from adolescence to adulthood a goal is to find one's own standpoint, to be able to make choices and decisions and be master in one's own house. Self-motivation and self-regulation can be nurtured, more or less, through practical activities in which pupils experience the resistance offered by different materials. Examples include glasswork, woodturning, metalwork and wool work. By stepping into the shoes of the student and experiencing what tensions the encounter with the material brings, we can understand the educational value of the activity and hence devise good learning activities. Among other things, we can create stimulating learning arenas for those youngsters who may be unable to realize their educational potential through conventional schooling.

Craft-based special education in the UK

Ruskin Mill

At Ruskin Mill Trust's (RMT) colleges in England, local craftspeople function both as teachers and special educators across a broad spectrum of practical learning arenas. Here, handicraft and agriculture have become an educational-therapeutic instrument for young people (aged 17–26) struggling with learning and social disabilities. Skills such as attention, coordination, motor skills, concentration and social interaction can be honed in a

At Ruskin Mill, special education, ecological stewardship and local enterprise hand in hand. At the fish farm, tutor Aron shows the students how they can kill the fish with respect before it is processed and smoked at the smokery and then served in the cafe, or vacuum packed for sale at the college shop. Photograph by Jorunn Barane.

self-motivated and self-regulated process that works along two dimensions. *Internally*, it involves those self-regulating processes which the resistance of the material demands. Ploughing with horses, for example, requires one to be fully present in oneself while simultaneously connecting with the horse. If a student does this for a whole day, the horse will give them something in return. A silent reciprocal dialogue takes place.

At Ruskin Mill College in Gloucestershire, an entire valley has been made into an arena for entrepreneurial learning in combination with sustainable education. Crafts people run their businesses in combination with education, so that what students produce with them in their workshops has a commercial dimension. They can make real commodities from the distinctive qualities and resources of their environment. In exchanges with customers, students gain respectful feedback about the process behind the products they have made. An example is the college's fish farm, where trout are reared, fished and packed to be sold at the farmer's market by the students themselves. Through the entrepreneurial work in the valley they engage in the maintenance of the landscape, horticulture, forestry and farming. This external therapeutic dimension situates the work they take part in in a holistic, ecological and social context.

Ruskin Mill Trust has five crafts-based special education colleges and 800 employees in the UK. The trust has been accorded Beacon Status by the national Learning and Skills Improvement Service (LSIS). In 2005 its founder, Aonghus

Gordon, was named Social Entrepreneur of the Year for the South of England.

Since 1986, thousands of students have taken part in RMT's 'Practical Skills Therapeutic Education', whose conceptual and methodological inspiration derives from John Ruskin, William Morris and Rudolf Steiner. The aim is to build up a range of practical learning spaces and workshops where young people with special needs can develop self-efficacy by learning new skills and mastering difficult processes.

RMT's vision is to give each student individual, meaningful experience of themselves and society, a prerequisite for being able to shape their own future. Learning programmes are underpinned by the belief that everyone has the potential for positive change and personal development. Activities are designed to integrate emotions, intellectual capacities, relational skills and practice. This requires openness, a positive attitude, and tolerance and respect towards others. Holistic learning and experience are facilitated through art, craft, entrepreneurship, agriculture, nutrition and health.

For more information, see: www.rmt.org.uk

Ruskin Mill works with hands, head and heart. The staff equip their students with tools so they can transform material and at the same time themselves. Having a productive impact on their surroundings empowers students as real participants in society. For many, this knowledge means the start of a new life.

FOR REFLECTION:
What does 'knowledge' mean within my subject area? And how can schools develop it in an inclusive way?

CHAPTER EIGHT

COOPERATION

A common social arena

'We have too many half-wise heads and not enough wise hands' – Lena Lindgren, social affairs editor for the *Morgenbladet* newspaper (2014, p. 40), is concerned that a society that does not value practical knowledge will be incapable of building quality from within. Since antiquity, morality has been deeply rooted in the concept of practice. Manual work and the trades are moral acts. Ethics is not an elective, an academic subject to study; it is something that we do. Are not such ethics in practice also the bedrock of any safe and sustainable social community? They are goals not just for schools but for all of us as lifelong learners.

In Chapter 4, we told of a journey into the world to find self-understanding, and of how, to understand the world, we must go into ourselves. In Chapter 5, we linked being creative to the act of opening ourselves to the future and stepping into the flow of time; to connect to, and see with our hearts, the needs of others. As we shall explore in Chapter 10, being an integrated person involves a number of contradictory aims: to develop independence but also the ability to function and work as a team, or 'to nurture the individual's uniqueness and to jointly contribute to society and its growth' (NCC 1997, p. 21). In Chapter 6, we saw how the values of bread emerge in the art of baking; a transformation is brought about by the way a person's hands have kneaded the dough. Serving high-quality local food in pleasant surroundings is a community-building end in itself. And creating such fine meeting places with warmth and consideration also contributes to a safe and sustainable social community.

Can place and landscape also become a meeting ground that we can all hold in common, unconditionally and irrespective of religious or cultural affiliation? Does building an inclusive society depend on us cooperating to develop and take responsibility for the landscape, nature, place or region we inhabit? Can a new and local, global responsibility for the environment pave the way for a new cultural diversity? These questions can be asked at different levels. Wherever there is fragmentation and division, including the divisions imposed between school subjects, it's possible to use place, its resources and landscape, as an integrating element. This can be done through practical activities such as planting flowers or fruit trees, sprucing things up, caring for our surroundings. Fellowship thereby gets rooted in practice, in doing something tangible together that strengthens community and the prospect of a sustainable future. So much fellowship can be found in following a little seed's progress into a plant and then selling it to a nice lady in the market square. Just ask the girl from Class 5 the day she says, 'This is the best day of my life!'.

Common values and visions

How to work together and look in the same direction without letting go of individuals' distinctive contributions? When we first began to lay out the school garden in 1994, we asked the caretaker to move the fence so as to create a safe outdoor space for the youngest classes. The garden was meant to be a place where children could actively engage and be inspired in their play by seeing that adults have tasks that they can emulate and interact with. The pupils were invited to help with the transformation of their outdoor surroundings. What did they expect of an outside area? What did they want? In the process that followed, pupils shared their ideas about what might be important aspects of their schoolyard. There were many good suggestions and drawings of running water, animals and flowers, and exciting slides and climbing frames.

In early spring it was time in the classroom to plan the garden for the coming season. Which plants should be sown? What did they look like? What did they smell and taste like? And what could they be used for? All this had to be visualized if the garden was to be. But the little designers did not have free run of the space; the garden had to be part of a wider story and involve the other classes as well. So the children had to find their place in the community. Similarly, the plants needed to fit into a context of rotation and interplanting – not least in the school schedule.

Parents were urged to join the spring preparations, and readily turned up with work clothing and tools; it was a great way to get parents involved in school life. Sedentary parents' evenings miss the mark in many ways; outside, it is easier to get acquainted, and parents can bring much practical knowledge.

Children today no longer have much access to the practical work of adults, and young people are excluded from processes in real life and have little say or responsibility. Consumption of mass media puts them in the role of passive spectators and so reinforces the tendency to withdraw into self-absorption.

Social sustainability

In the first year, a small garden took form. We were still feeling our way and were wary of taking on more than we could handle. That autumn the crop was good, with big pumpkins, fine flowers and tasty peas, and other class teachers asked to join in. Next season we extended the garden a little, and four years later we had three gardens: one each for the youngest, the middle years and the older ones. It is important to explore the feasibility of the project both among teachers and parents, and in terms of the ongoing activities of farm and place. 'It is important to exploit the school as a community of work for the development of social skills. It must be structured in such a way that the learners' activities have consequences for others, and so that they can learn from the impact of their decisions.' (NCC 1997, p. 40)

In this fashion we created spaces for learning and extended their scope to include the valley, outfields and mountains. Before long we needed additional expertise, so we established agreements with the Mountain Ranger Office, local organizations and businesses in the district. Kvaløy Setreng (2014), for whom 'meaningful work' is the foundation of sustainability, predicts that social sustainability will come to outweigh economic sustainability. That's because capital must be regulatable at a local level (ibid., p. 130). Social sustainability is thus an important condition for creating an attractive local community where people will want to live.

Creating value in meeting

Through cross-boundary cooperation and organization, our place and the school have become a forum for new knowledge and experience, voluntary work, new acquaintances and networks. Parents have pitched in to help with the schoolyard, making benches and laying flowerbeds. Every spring they help to dig over the school garden and in summer they help with weeding and watering. At other times they lend a hand in the outfields, clearing woodland, cutting wood or building cabins. We cook soup over a fire, make coffee and eat biscuits, often with a musical interlude or two. In his account of relational pedagogy, Spurkeland stresses the ability to collaborate and equates it with 'relational competence', which he defines as 'skills, abilities, knowledge and attitudes that establish, develop, maintain and repair relationships between people' (2011, p. 63).

Place and landscape were our venue for creative collaboration and development. It turns out that it's easier to get to know both parents and teachers when you're doing something jointly. The sight of their parents and teachers creating something together means a lot for children's well-being.

According to Spurkeland (2011, p. 194), the most neglected and least exploited relationship in schools is that with the parents. Research shows that there is quite a gap between the ideal and the reality of cooperation between home and school (Nordahl 2007). At parents meetings in a classroom setting, teachers often have the floor and are the authority figures. During a work session in the schoolyard, however, the roles can reverse; here it might be a parent, or an uncle, say, who has the know-how to take charge of building benches. It's important to view both parents and grandparents as resources and to use them as such more often. The dimensions of relational pedagogy that Spurkeland (2011) proposes can readily be extended from the indoor arena of school to encompass relationships that pupils and school form with the local community and with culture and nature at large.

Place as an arena for interdisciplinary cooperation

Interdisciplinary schoolwork starts with a central project in which different subjects can fit. Any language subject can link to any kind of work-based experience. Maths can similarly be applied to concrete exercises in the field, through measuring, weighing, calculating areas, etc. In the natural sciences, it's desirable to explore particular places in detail in order to familiarize pupils with different biotopes – coast, mountains, forest, etc. Nature in all its shifting aspects around the year can also stitch together what is learnt in the various science subjects: geology, soil science, botany, zoology and ecology. Contact with nature through the seasons can give pupils an understanding not just of a system, but of a dynamic whole. Everything in nature is moving: something dies and turns to soil so that something else may grow. In certain landscapes, growth proceeds slowly, as in the mountains. Other landscapes and biotopes – the river, say – are more dynamic. A living knowledge of the dynamic, ever-changing quality of nature is a condition for understanding and stewarding it.

All schools should give pupils a vivid introduction to the natural history of the place they have grown up in. Such a living sense of natural history cannot be imparted unless we go out and witness and experience processes and connections in the landscape.

Place is also where natural history and cultural history can be combined in one picture. One can trace this interplay in all local history. Social studies and history are eminently suited to using place as a learning arena. As we have shown, one will find stories and themes that tie in with the core of the subject. When planning curriculum, one can link different subjects and school years to holistic topics and projects that pupils will work with over long periods of time. In sports, physical motion and outdoor life can be combined. Craft subjects are few and far between in today's schools, but they too can be revived in projects relating to the use of natural resources and traditional handicrafts in the local community.

Any number of cooperative projects can emerge from combining arts subjects with more theoretical subjects. Drawing and painting are well suited for both the natural sciences and language; they teach you to see, which requires more than taking a quick snapshot.

Last but not least, place is a venue for cooperative learning. Cooperation is founded on there being a concrete task to work on jointly; we create something that has purpose and that means something – and we do it together, cooperating. Cooperative learning in school becomes lopsided when it involves only cognitive cooperation. Through more comprehensive development of the venues that we invite pupils into, we can develop a more comprehensive culture of cooperation – where different types of abilities are valued and practised.

The school grounds as a community meeting place

A person's abilities and identity evolve through interaction with the outside world. Human beings shape their local surroundings even as these surroundings shape them. Local communities with their working life and the encompassing natural world are a vital part of a school's learning environment. Youngsters derive from them experiences and impulses that teaching should celebrate and make use of. School leaders must reach out to the neighbourhood and mobilize the resources in the school's surroundings. 'The school shall function as an active source of energy and culture for the local community, and promote not only contact between adults and children, but also with local services and industry' (NCC 1997, p. 18).

Efforts to open the school to participating in the local community will be enhanced by opening its doors as an arena for community and parent participation. In our work to develop the school grounds and garden, described above, parents were key actors. Less formal and more hands-on contexts like these provide a frame and a reason to socialize. The school garden is a good example of how such arenas can become a meeting place for the local community. Parents were invited to join in with the work of building the garden, the community benefits from the products grown there, and the solidarity project Nina Children Home[5] in Kenya makes a link to the wider world.

FOR REFLECTION:

How can place facilitate cooperation between subjects? How can the school grounds be opened up to be a meeting place for the local community?

CHAPTER NINE

ENVIRONMENTAL AWARENESS

Local ecology

> According to legend, the renowned fiddler Lisbet-Per, who lived in the 1700s, was on his way down the Nærøy Valley when he chanced upon a huldre bridal procession.[6] Per threw his fire steel over the bride, making her stop while the procession continued on. He proceeded to rob her, first of her silver finery, and then her clothes. The bride had been silent, but now she beseeched him: could she not keep what little she had left? But Per took both her brooch and her shift, and so lost his power over her. But before the bride went into the hill, she turned to Per and said: 'Because of your cruelty, your offspring will be marked in body or soul for nine generations. Then your family will die out for ever.'

Lisbet-Per's huldre silver is widely scattered. The wreath went to Luster; a few clasps are in Voss; the piece shown below was long in the possession of Sussi Sivle Collett, but in 1953 she presented a collection of 100 items, inherited from her father, to the municipality of Aurland, and among them was the huldre brooch. Sussi Sivle Collett says, 'Its spell should be broken now. I am in the ninth generation from Lisbet-Per and I have no descendants.'

The huldre folklore of Indre Sogn is formed in the tension between local ecology and culture, says Christensen (2000) in his book *Bergteken* [Taken by the Mountain]. The stories tell of the mixed blessing of interdependence. People had little choice but to help each other in very many areas of daily life, and those who did not conform put themselves outside the accepted social structures – to the detriment of both themselves and the community. Stories in which the huldrefolk either help or punish and do harm can be understood as commentaries on the positive as well as the problematic aspects of community. Natural resources were a common good. Nobody can help themselves at the expense of the community without there being consequences.

Depending on our reading, these narratives can either signify relationships between humans and huldrefolk or relationships among humans. The latter interpretation lets us lift the stories out of history and see their timeless meaning.

Huldre brooch, on display in the Sivle collection at the Local History Centre in Aurland. Photograph: Thor Andresen.

> We must accept the tension between myth and science and make a fruitful balance between them. Science corrects myth by preventing us from getting lost in delusion, while myth corrects the blindness of science to human responsibility and the meaning of life. (Dahlin 2004, p. 123)

How has humankind's relationship to nature changed over history? In the story of our shifting place in the world we can discern lines of development which can help us approach the future today. Our view of nature has changed over the course of time. If we are to understand ourselves and the problems our culture has with the environment, we need a historical perspective. We must understand the lines of development in which we are participating.

Conceptions of nature across time

> The aim of education is to influence people's way of thinking and enable them to make the world more equitable and sustainable; to contribute to critical reflection and increased awareness; and to provide the knowledge necessary to develop new methods and tools. (Utdanningsdirektoratet 2012, p. 8)

There is a close connection between how we think, deep down, and how we act towards nature. With this as his starting point, Hjalmar Hegge (1993) enquires into the connections between our conceptions of nature and our practical dealings with it. What affinities and what differences are there between humans and nature? After all, Hegge says, 'nature is much more than a material basis for human life; it is a part of us and we are a part of it' (ibid., pp. 117–141). How to understand this relation and how it has been understood at different times are therefore vital questions. A number of ecologists point out that nature provides not only sustenance for our physical bodies, but also essential nourishment of our inner life: 'Being our material world around us, it is the obvious place for our senses to unfold, which nourish our emotional development in an essential way' (ibid., p. 11).

The age of myth

In the age of myth we find no 'theory' of nature; rather it comes to expression in art and poetry. Nature is understood through images recognizable to us from, say, the Norse and Greek myths and legends. Is this thinking so very alien to us today? In culture and tradition, we know such culture-bearing narratives from the imagery of fairy tales and in art and poetry. They recall experiences and mental representations children have before they are capable of logical thought. But today we have the caveat that these images aren't to be understood as actually real. We regard them as subjective fantasy products of children, artists and myth. To find the truth in nature today, one is supposed to steer clear of such fantasies – and see objectively what nature really is. In the age of myth there was no sharp divide between humans and nature. People felt more at one with nature; they did not keep it at arm's length. The world, or nature, they perceived as umbilically linked to their own being; the 'self' was part of the world and the world was part of the soul.

Just as infants are still one with the world around them, not because of any consideration on their part but because of their way of being in it, so there was no distinction between people's immediate experience of the world and their understanding of it. Experience of the world and the inner life seemed to be more or less two sides of the same thing. People related lightning and thunder, clouds drifting across the sky, sunshine and the movements of the stars to the moods and forces they experienced within themselves. In the age of myth the power and might of the sea were not merely properties of nature, but properties of the human soul. In fleeting poetic moments we can feel something similar today, but the difference is that we think it is simply a subjective quality in us. We would not say that nature is a carrier of soul qualities. The divine entities we know from mythology were just as present in nature as they were in the human soul. Thus, moral qualities were ascribed to both nature and humans. People regarded nature as they would a relative, because they understood and experienced it in terms of themselves. From a moral perspective this means that a person knows that harming nature is tantamount to self-harm. Such a way of understanding nature warranted careful interaction with it. Today we are starting to see the rightness of such an attitude, which offers a rationale for what we would now call ecologically sound living.

Nature as model and ideal

The mythical form of experiencing the world continued through much of antiquity. The advent of the first philosophers and conceptual thinking came quite late. These early philosophers regarded thinking as intimately linked to the world, which was seen as a web of living relationships. The balance is therefore easily disturbed. The overall experience of an animated, living nature survived, although the mythic way of understanding gradually disappeared. So nature is still understood to be something that humans are part of and not separate from. The difference is that this view now draws on philosophical concepts and rational argument, as in the great classical thinkers Plato and Aristotle. Here we see the birth of independence in thought.

The Greeks' departure from mythical consciousness had two sides. The first was something they found tragic; we can call it 'isolation' – the sense of having severed the relation to nature and the spiritual in nature that earlier cultures had; of having lost a connection to one's origins. The second was liberating, the exhilaration of being able to think freely, with thought its own foundation, independent of the experiences or traditions that gave rise to it. According to Hegge (1989), the philosophy that was born in Greece is characterized by the liberation of thinking – a new ability to function freely and independently from experience – to become conscious of itself.

According to Hegge, the philosophy that was born in Greece is characterized by the liberation of thinking – a new ability to think freely and independently of experience – and, accompanying this liberation of thinking, a strengthened self-conscious self.

For Plato the source of ideas lies in the spiritual world, detached from the world we sense with our physical senses. For Aristotle the source of human understanding lies in the encounter with the sensuous world. This polarity between the Platonic and Aristotelian worldviews is a key to understanding the further development of the philosophy of nature in Europe. The result in late antiquity was separation and dualism in the relationship between the human being and nature. The kinship between the human being and nature which permeates thought in antiquity, and all human experience in the age of myth, was now beginning to break apart. This separation also implies a separation between the sacred and spiritual realm and nature. Problems relating to this double separation, between the human being and nature, on one hand, and between God and nature, on the other, was pivotal to medieval philosophy and culture (Hegge 1993).

Outer and inner nature

In the transition to the Middle Ages there's a splitting between inner and outer nature. On one hand, there's the notion of an ideal nature that is perceived as purely internal because it never manifests visibly. On the other hand, we have visible, external nature, now seen as directly counteracting the ideal, true nature, because it prevents the ideal world from emerging. At this time in Christendom people were expected to seek the supersensible world. The natural world, on earth, was wicked, and humankind should only engage with it to secure the essentials to sustain life. An alternative view was that, although the supersensible was paramount, all nature was nonetheless the work of God and therefore worthy of respect.

Medieval thinkers such as Thomas Aquinas and Albertus Magnus built on Aristotle's thought and claimed that to occupy oneself with God's creation was to serve him – we should seek the Lord through his creation. This was echoed by Francis of Assisi and his attitude towards living things: people should not only find their own salvation on earth, but also contribute to the spiritualization and salvation of all creation. We find the same idea in German romanticism, as when Novalis speaks of man as the redeemer of nature (Hegge 1993, p. 66).

Our time

But this was not the understanding that would be passed on to our time. Instead, the view prevailed that man is nature's master, entitled to dominate it for his own ends. This would not have been possible without there being a parallel shift in our conception of nature. With the transition to modern times a further separation occurs between the inner experience and outer nature. The real world is material. And the things that people previously experienced in the soul and in nature – image-producing, vital and aesthetic qualities such as colours, tones and fragrances – are now labelled as purely subjective: they become secondary sensory qualities. Instead of a holistic view of human beings and the world, there is an unbridgeable gulf between them. It is dead world, devoid of qualities the human being can either identify with or feel at home with. It turns out – and here Hegge is back where he started – that how we think is closely related to how we act towards nature. In the age of myth, people were one with nature and acted accordingly. Today, we must be able to *both* unite with nature and see it from outside *with awareness.* To know something about the world, we must both step back from and at the same time be involved in it.

From ego to eco

> We live increasingly on the surface – we consume to be seen. The systems that profit from this are those tormenting nature and people around the world. The systems are dependent on our dependence. (Haukeland 2008, pp. 1–2)

One of the most important things we can do in today's complex world is to create learning situations that cultivate the ability to make connections and see contexts. The philosopher Arne Næss (1912–2009) called on us to pause and ask ourselves if we really want to provide for such situations. He wanted us to reconsider what direction we are taking, individually and collectively. Deep experiences give our lives direction, meaning and content; they ignite a spark in us. Næss also talks of a deeper Self (with a capital 'S'), or, in his words, an 'expanded' or 'extended Self' (Haukeland 2008). He says the Self must be understood as something expanded to include the whole that we are part of. Everything the individual is part of is thus – in widening circles – a part of the individual.

In saying this, Næss emphasizes that people cannot succeed without also actualizing that which they are a part of. The whole we are part of must be actualized if we are to actualize ourselves. This is to gain a type of insight that makes it possible to live a full human life. Arne Næss and many others in the so-called 'deep ecology' movement have been inspired by the philosophy of Spinoza – in particular his view of God and nature, but also his account of reason and feeling. According to Næss, Spinoza's view of human beings is such that he believes negative emotions never capture us completely. They make us passive, but there's something in us that always tries to bring out our positive emotions, and these activate the whole person. Arne Næss says that Spinoza links this something to the word *ratio*.

For Spinoza, *ratio* indicates a deeper 'reason' that is tied to who we are and what we stand for deep down. It is an inner voice that tells us whether or not a choice of action is in accord with our nature. Spinoza links his concept of God to the creative principle in nature, a creative force in all living beings. That is to say, God is not a being who once created the world. God is the living force at work in us and in nature, right here and now. This force shows us what it's possible to achieve as creative and positive forces in the world.

Society today is often characterized by *narrow reason* and techno-economic goals that frame what is possible and economically viable and what there is political will to implement. When measured against clean air, ecological sustainability, reduced noise pollution and better health, this may turn out to be *deeply irrational* in the long term with respect to quality of life and sustainability.

Dialogue between place and learning

At SJH one of the core subjects is processing local raw materials. After pupils have gone through the various techniques – cheese-making, milking, cultivation and drying of herbs, plant dyes, growing and weaving of flax, slaughtering sheep and smoking mountain trout – they may pick a topic or product for in-depth study. They have to document the process and present this at the end of term. One year, two boys chose pig slaughtering as their topic. They would buy two piglets and rear them for six months until they reached a carcass weight of 75 kg. Here is their story.

Pig slaughter

The boys bought two piglets in the neighbouring village and built them a home of straw bales in the field. Straw insulates well in winter so the piglets were comfortable, and they were well looked after. An electric fence was set up around the straw house. The pigs grew fit and strong, till one fine day they were able to clear the fence. Later in winter, with Christmas approaching, the farmer himself thought it was high time to slaughter them. He shook his head at the effort of catching them when they escaped. Somehow the two boys managed to delay the slaughter until after the Christmas holidays. The pigs now had to be moved to a taller enclosure at the back of the barn, where the young animals usually go.

I had watch duty that week. Each night I had to make the rounds and turn out the lights. That was when I saw a light was on in the stable and went to investigate. By the enclosure, I could hear low voices in the darkness. Getting closer I saw two youths, each with an arm around a pig – grown big by now.

'What are you doing here?', I asked. 'It's cold and dark.'

'It's their last night', was their reply.

Early the next morning I saw they had put everything in order. They lit a large fire in the yard – boiling water was needed to rinse the pigs. The local slaughterman had already arrived and the slaughtering mask had been brought out. The pigs did not make a sound. The mood in the tun was solemn. The whole landscape watched and held its breath. This being January, it started to snow, light snowflakes covering the green slopes, smoke rising from the fire.

That day I had some extra chores to do in the nursery, but I was curious to follow events. The next time I came out, the pigs hung high from the loader. The snow had settled and one of the boys stood stirring the blood to prevent it from coagulating. I could hear the deep conversation between the two in the expectant, quiet atmosphere of the tun. The sight of smoke rising from the fire evoked an act of sacrifice, the feeling that a holy rite had been performed.

What I saw and learnt was this: that if you are really attached to what you are doing, you give something back to your setting. You give a part of yourself. We discussed this during the lunch break. Several others had experienced the same thing. Some of the teachers were troubled, concerned whether the pupils had been too self-directed today. They had meant to help and teach them about the different parts of the pig but had been prevented from doing so.

In the evening I did my rounds again. This time the fire house lights were on, and when I opened the door the two boys were sitting there on crates. Between them was a tub of water with a pig's head floating in it. The boys were stuffing the cleaned intestines, and from a wooden rod in the ceiling hung strings of fine sausages. The profound conversation between them had resumed. Not wanting to disturb them, I closed the door and stole way. The following day there was a poster on the outer door inviting dog owners to pop in and get some free bones. In other words, the work was done.

Inner and outer sensitivity

Looking at the pupils' process, we see that it takes two tracks, one internal and one external. In the *outer* track we see the process from piglets all the way to the final cuts. The pupils' learning path goes via skills and connections that are integral to the process of rearing a pig for meat. Through participation in the process they learn to master each step and understand the necessary conditions. By following the path and learning the requirements for each step, they develop competence and understanding. In terms of the subject's learning objectives, the pupils are completing a journeyman exam – whose steps they must follow. At the end of it, everything is processed and made into products; nothing is wasted. Apprenticeship learning is about getting inside the process to experience its inherent lawfulness. There is an ethic in all processes which able craftspeople understand, regardless of specialty. The ethic is inextricable from the way the work is performed.

According to Krogh (2010), the experience of skilled insight into the underlying pattern of a process can be a key skills qualification that is transferable to other fields. We learn a craft, we learn something specific, but we also acquire abilities and qualities that have general relevance. What key skills qualifications have the pupils acquired? Some are transferable skills, while others involve transferable understanding. The former relate to practical participation; the latter depend on the thought following action. The specific requirements for carrying out this task are: knowing the law as regards slaughter and meat production; knowing when in the year slaughter is permitted; being able to meet the animal with respect and getting to know your own reaction to the encounter with killing; consciously relating to the question of taking life for food; knowledge about hygiene and the place of slaughter, and avoiding contact with soil; familiarity with the work environment and slaughtering tools; awareness of animal ethics; dexterity; precision during the slaughter moment; anatomical knowledge in butchering; and compliance with rules for waste disposal.

Interlaced with this outer track is an *inner* track linking to education. There is gravitas in this part of the path, which deepens as the pupils progress. Here we are touching the core: forming an attachment to animals and parting from them; life and death. All people are born with the ability to connect with the world, and this ability is linked to our deepest humanity. At the same time, it is precisely this ability which makes us vulnerable. To touch and be touched, move and be moved, is a necessary condition for our creative awakening. In art we know that expression is deepened when the practitioners themselves are moved by it. In this light, the slaughter story raises interesting questions: did this 'work' also become great because its performers were moved by the great cycle they were immersed in?

The creative power in human beings and nature

Spring Night in the Garden by Nikolai Astrup (1909) shows us the ensouled moon reflecting in Jølstravatnet, building a bridge between heaven and earth. The garden is no longer just a place for work. The atmosphere and stillness in the image lead us beyond the practical work with the soil. The small field becomes a holy place. The landscape lies in a dream light that both illuminates and hides. Humans are part of a bigger context than the one they have made themselves. Depictions of nature were not just depictions of local landscapes and living conditions. They are signs that, when decoded, remind us that the near and the concrete always bear within them something larger, an eternal dimension of life that is at once spiritual and material (Danbolt *et al.* 2005, p. 94).

Nikolai Astrup. Spring night in the garden, 1909. Photograph©: O. Væring Eftf. AS

CHAPTER TEN

INTEGRITY

Being human is not something we simply *are*, with a set of categories we can agree about and be done with. It is something we gradually become through personal development. Human beings are created to be creators also of themselves. Within every pupil, but also within every teacher, we find this inner drive. Human beings are created to learn, say Dahlin and colleagues (2002). There is a meaning to life, and we tend to forget this. As well as to *know*, to *do* and to *live together*, we must learn to simply *be*, Dahlin observes, because to learn to be is to learn to love, not just what attracts us, but *all that there is* – existence, our surroundings and the world as a whole.

The swing between becoming and belonging

Humans can be understood as 'becoming beings'. We come into existence through our *participation* in the world. To the extent that we are deprived of important aspects of this participation, we are deprived of conditions to develop important sides of our own humanity and genius (Hüter 2004). *Belonging* in the world is also something we only find through this participation. We grow closer to what we see and sense, shape, work with and understand. If pedagogy is to be human, it must put itself at the service of this double mission: to develop learning spaces that allow each individual to stretch out and *unfold their branches* and at the same time *put down their roots* in the local community. The moment schools and teachers take such pedagogy seriously enough to put it into effect, they are, in ethical terms, agents of social development.

If we look at the six aspects of human potential in the preceding chapters, a common motif seems to be the breathing between productive mode of will at work (*volition*) and receptive mode of sensing (*belonging*). In spiritual learning activities, creative expression and practically oriented work, we grow into connections through our interest. Self-drive is initiated (Hugo 1995). Through cognitive, emotional or intentional self-drive the ability to connect with the world in turn gets strengthened. A double waveform arises in this pendulum motion – from the inside out, and from the outside in. The outside that we encounter is breathed in; the inside that we think is exhaled. The wave resembles what occurs in verbal dialogues when a conversation is underway. Just as in a good conversation, it undulates back and forth. The meeting between outward and inward movement creates a third entity, a space and a question about the way ahead. When we see what such a dialogue means – in the meeting between outside and inside – we have arrived at a *living concept of learning*.

The main task of the educator is no longer to steer down predefined routes to predefined outcomes, but to help initiate this dialogue between self-volition and connection, to give air to the meeting between that which is taken in and that which is let out. We may glimpse here the alternation between sleep and wakefulness, participation and rest, impression and expression. Teachers can train a sensitivity to the breathing between working with connection and working with self-drive. When planning lessons, we therefore need to train our eyes to see the potential for self-drive and connection that's present in what a task demands and what it gives.

It's clear from this simple formula that integrated human beings are only conceivable in relation to their environment. The promotion by schools of the 'decontextualized classroom' as a universal arena is pushed by an instrumental concept of learning which fragments the ecology of knowing. Just as we now recoil at the sight of a caged tiger bereft of all habitat, so future educators will react to the sight of a person who has been dislodged from their topos, their place in the world.

Practical work needs thought

All practical work needs thought: we must use our heads in order to accomplish practical tasks well. Conversely, recent neurobiology (Spitzer 1999; Hüter 2004) can now show that the physiological development of the brain depends on sensory, linguistic and motor activity, and that this is *weakened* when sensory, physical contact with the world is restricted (Sigman 2010). Cognitive development is intimately linked to the early stages of physical development. We can thus comprehend how the different forms of knowledge in a person fit together into an integrated whole. Where thought is unable to progress on its own it receives help from the hands, which can try things out. If a task is to be carried out smoothly in practice, it must be complemented by conscious planning, evaluation and adjustment to the situation. All practical work, in its choices and processes, is accompanied by thinking. The skilled craftsperson thinks through processes and visualizes them.

Here, it is the will that gives us connection with our task, while thought gives us distance. We solve a practical task through a silent dialogue between entering it with our will and stepping out from it with our thinking. As we grow in competence we become able to let the two processes run in parallel: we can accompany the activity with a conscious stream of free judgement. This combination of being completely absorbed in a task and at the same time consciously penetrating it is similar to what Donald Schön calls the 'zone of mastery' in his book *The Reflective Practitioner* (1984). Through actively accompanying an area of activity, thinking can learn to become focused and strong enough to respond to the immediate needs of the moment. According to Dreyfus and Dreyfus (1986), this is the hallmark of the expert level of skill. What the master architect and the master cellist have in common is that they are completely absorbed by what they are doing and at the same time able to act independently and make intuitive decisions. When thinking and action complement each other in this way, they become a 'feel' for the subject. In sport we speak of a 'feel for the ball' where thinking is at one with doing. Similarly, mastery in maths or chess implies a level of 'professional intuition' or 'instinct'; when performed this is recognizable (as in artistic performance) as genius or style. Here we see the impetus from work with head and hand to creative expression. If we have got inside what we are seeing and doing, then we too have the opportunity to give it a 'personal touch'.

It is this sense of mastery that we aspire to nurture in children and young people. All children and young people, regardless of background and impediment, bear within them the potential to develop such connection and release in practical and social activity.

Illeris (2013, p. 163) says that 'competence' should encompass what one is able to do in practice: it's not just what one has learnt that counts; it is what one does with it. He quotes Per Schultz Jørgensen, a professor in social psychology: 'The concept of competence refers ... to a person's being qualified in a broader sense. It is not merely that a person masters a professional area, but also that the person can apply this professional knowledge – and more than that, apply it in relation to the requirements inherent in a situation which, in addition, may be uncertain and unpredictable.' Thus the concept includes the person's judgements, attitudes and ability to draw upon their personal conclusions (Jørgensen and Phillips 1999, p. 4). Illeris adds that there are many elements that are not yet included in prevailing concepts of competence: making appropriate judgements and decisions, seeing the big picture, understanding things from a structural perspective, overview, sociality and the ability to collaborate, independence, self-insight and self-confidence, and a personal motive. Beyond this are yet more crucial elements to take into account. First, in the creative area: creativity, imagination, the faculty of combination and flexibility. Second, in the interpersonal area: empathy and intuition. Third, in the critical area: a critical approach and the potential for resistance (Illeris 2013).

We connect to the world through our senses

If we take a closer look at how we locate ourselves in the world in scholarly, creative or practical pursuits, we are led back to the silent dialogue between sensing and thinking. We connect to the world through our senses. Just as plants can't exist without being connected through their roots, so people are rooted in dialogue with the world through their senses (Holdrege 2014). Meeting the world inspires wonder. We comprehend what we experience, with names, concepts and understanding. As children we live this process quite naturally, by encountering experiences that speak to all of our senses. The senses also have the ability to integrate our experience; they weave together so that we hear, see and smell as an integrated whole. It involves our senses of touch, movement, warmth, smell, taste, sight and, gradually, a sense of language and an ability to sense the uniqueness of our surroundings. As we grow, our thinking is empowered and can release itself from what we are experiencing. It takes on a dynamic of its own and gradually gains independence. We can make our own judgements and decisions based on what we ourselves believe to be right.

The ability to be independent and morally autonomous stems from the ability to participate in the world – independence and the ability to take responsibility evolve hand in hand. We don't turn into ethically acting people in an instant; rather we have the potential to become them, provided we have the chance to connect to the world. Through connection and attachment we are able to practise releasing ourselves so that our thinking grows strong enough to make us clear-sighted and independent individuals. Only when we take responsibility for this process, that is, for our own thinking and for what we consider to be right and wrong, do we become truly creative human beings.

This point lies at the core of Gert Biesta's (2006) critique of the instrumental language of learning and the thinking behind it. To weigh and measure every aspect of learning without grasping that education is about becoming is devastating, he argues. If we lose sight of the connection to human development and only measure components of what we acquire and how we perform, as if a person were a system to be 'optimized', then no space will be left for the actual person, or for the process that should be central to all education, namely that of becoming. A defining human characteristic is precisely this ability to keep growing and not to rigidify in a frozen form of knowledge.

New beginnings

The teaching profession today is often stressful and burnout levels are high. Why, Bo Dahlin (2010) asks, is this the case? Could it be because belief in one's own values, humanity and meaning, beauty and love, must defer to economic forces and management by targets? When both pupils and teachers are reduced to instruments with which to achieve objectives, the very basis for the teacher as a fount of ethical awareness crumbles away: 'Present neoliberal educational policies may contribute to such erosions of the conditions of possibility of ethical action in educational practice' (Dahlin 2010, p. 1).

Biesta argues along similar lines. Criticizing the new production-based 'language of learning' in schools, he notes its striking similarities to the market model for delivering goods and services. When such a conceptual apparatus is armed with instruments for monitoring and controlling delivery, there's a risk of forgetting that human beings' development is at stake: 'Any attempt to make education into a technique, any attempt to conceive of it in terms of instrumentality, poses a threat to the very possibility of becoming somebody through education' (Biesta 2006, p. 70).

Biesta takes up philosopher Hannah Arendt's (1977) thoughts on human growth. Here the neoliberal argument that it all comes down to mastery is turned on its head: for Arendt, incompleteness is the sine qua non of the human condition; it is the prerequisite for the human capacity to grow, to keep making new beginnings. 'Our impossibility to remain unique masters of what we do, that is at the very same time the condition – and the only condition – under which our beginnings can come into the world' (Arendt 1977, p. 220).

Through 'new beginnings' a person grows step by step into the world. Year by year we expand our fields of interest and practice. The most important ethical responsibility for schools and teachers is to create space for just such individual and constant 'new beginnings'.

Theodor Kittelsen. White Bear King Valemon and the golden wreath, 1912.
Photograph©: O. Væring Eftf. AS

PART III

ECOPRENEURSHIP IN EDUCATION

Photograph: Nat Mead

> I shall never rest until I know that all my ideas are derived, not from hearsay or tradition, but from my real living contact with the things themselves. (Goethe 1970, p. 347)

How can schools become creative centres for sustainable community development? The questions we deal with in this book address the shaping of a partnership whereby schools open up to participate in life, and life opens up its potential for education. The stories we tell and the tools we present may be seen as stepping stones towards the formation of 'spaces of education' we have yet to imagine. These may in the end differ radically from what we today consider to be typical schools or classrooms. Adopting a term coined by Goethe, we may call these places 'pedagogical provinces'.

Goethe's pedagogical provinces

In his novel *Wilhelm Meister's Apprenticeship*, Johann Wolfgang Goethe (1749–1832) presents a vision of the school of the future, which is not a 'school' in the common sense of the word, but rather comprises locations where formative education takes place. He names such places 'pedagogical provinces'. Their hallmark is proximity to life through layers of interactive relationships between nature and culture. Agricultural and horticultural work interconnects with handicraft and cultural activities. Equestrian skills are refined in parallel with musical education.

All arenas and activities are dedicated to educating the whole human being, making possible the versatile development of individual qualities and skills. Each province has its own profile, represented by a concord of activities and businesses adapted to the distinctiveness of the place and the people living there. This allows each adolescent to find an educational track corresponding to his or her potential. The pedagogical province sustains a balanced and diverse community of permanently residing professionals and visiting apprentices.

How can schools begin this process of engaging in local development? To a great extent, the answer is that designing and exploring local curricula *is* engagement in the development of the local environment and community. The shaping of place-based curricula is comparable to innovation processes in culture and business. It requires an open and searching attitude to how an inner idea or vision is to be realized in the outside world. The vision must build on a value base that is made explicit and at the same time can be shared by a wider community.

A starting point here is to agree that understanding the connections around us where we live is a basis for caring about and participating in democratic processes. In secondary school, the environmental and social subjects become relevant and alive to pupils when they link into aspects of their own situation in time and place. Here cross-disciplinary work is apt, since natural sciences, environmental studies and social sciences meet in the physical landscape. Subjects should not merely describe the state of things past and present; they should also facilitate discussion about new ways to achieve a more sustainable, locally and regionally rooted democracy.

CHAPTER ELEVEN

AN INTERNATIONALLY EMERGING MOVEMENT

Over the past twenty years, we have seen a growing crop of 'school stories' that have a certain resemblance to 'pedagogical provinces': schools where pupils encounter life – artisans, artists and agriculturists. The municipality of Aurland is just one example. Here, long-term dedicated pedagogical work with place-based curricula has given new impulses to the relationships between agriculture and community, place and school.

This process started in the 1990s with a garden for children at our primary and secondary school (ABU) on the grounds of the neighbouring agricultural college (SJH). From the school garden, the programme was gradually extended to encompass an increasing variety of learning spaces or 'arenas', from farmyard to pastures, woods, riverbeds and fjord, and the high mountains. The consistency of this approach in the school's curriculum is recognized in Norway as the 'Aurland model'. In recent years, the community of Aurland has gathered a network of professional resource people and institutions throughout Norway and elsewhere in Europe. One international partner is Ruskin Mill Trust (RMT) in the UK. With its diverse provinces of craft- and place-based educational centres for students with special needs, RMT is a vibrant example of how Goethe's idea can work in a modern research-based professional context.

The idea of place-based education is not new, nor is it limited to pedagogical visioning. Yet the complexity and alienation of modern life and the environmental challenges facing us call for fresh frameworks for integrated planning, heritage management and community development. Parallel to the awakening to new pedagogical platforms, there is also a broader trend towards regional awareness connected to the interrelationship between social and ecological systems (Wright et al. 2011).

From the local to the global: Mgeta's Friends

Lifting one's consciousness from the local to the global is not an uncommon exercise in our time. Through the media we receive images, sounds and stories from the whole world. The impressions are so many, so frequent and so overwhelming that a single event seldom makes a deep and lasting impression capable of changing our self-image, values, understanding or behaviour. Deeper changes usually build upon a longer pathway of development. Mental stimulation alone is not enough. To connect with a phenomenon, a theme or an activity, people usually need first to experience it as meaningful. The experience of emotional meaning awakens an interest that has two consequences. First, attention and will become focused on doing something that benefits whatever it is that gives meaning. Second, people will often want to understand the thing that has aroused their interest.

It is easiest to connect with people, activity and places where we live our daily lives. Our bodies give us admission to the world. Connection to our surroundings occurs through our senses and develops through our movements and skills. But it is, of course, possible to form a connection to far-away people, activities and places. Stories can help by making images of, and associations to, things that are distant or in the past. The storyteller becomes a bridge. If the storyteller has experienced something that is emotionally engaging, his or her ability to communicate it to others in a living way can prompt them to make their own connections. Just as important is the trust the listeners place in the storyteller. In the following, we give an example of how the global can become local through such a connection.

In Tanzania, 200 km west of the coastal city Dar es Salaam, a mountain chain rises steeply from the plain. The climate in the mountains is temperate, wet and suited to growing food on the terraces along the steep hillsides. For over three decades, NMBU and the Sokoine University of Agriculture in Tanzania have worked to introduce Norwegian dairy goats in the region of Mgeta in the Uluguru Mountains.[7] The Norwegian researchers' involvement in other local development projects includes setting up the NGO Mgeta's Friends.[8]

Mgeta's Friends promote the sustainable development of local communities so that both communities and individuals can become independent, rather than relying on foreign assistance. The people in the mountain villages are poor. The soil is depleted. Schools face a shortage of teachers, books and equipment that is taken for granted in Norway. The pupils come to school hungry and unable to concentrate for long. To address such needs and lay the foundations for self-reliance, the support of Norwegian donors was needed for a development phase.

Mgeta's Friends didn't simply ask for money; they chose a longer route to encourage potential donors to identify with the needs of the people in Mgeta. They first created connections to stimulate interest, then let individuals decide themselves whether to support the projects in the mountains. In 2010 they launched a project that aimed to empower orphans by loaning them goats. Hundreds of children in Mgeta have been orphaned by HIV/AIDS. Usually, they live with aunts, uncles or grandparents, but many live on their own. In their mid-teens they have to make their own living. Keeping a dairy goat could be a possible gateway to self-sufficiency. But in order to receive a goat the orphan first needed to build a goat shed.

The project was inspired by the maxim, 'Give a man a fish and you feed him for a day; teach a man to fish and you feed him for a lifetime'. Norwegian donors financed goat kids, building materials and the salary of the local coordinator, Solomon Mwakasumba. To strengthen the project's sustainability and the social responsibility among the orphans, every orphan had to pay back their goat loan by giving their first new-born female kid to a newcoming orphan goat farmer. Solomon instructed the pioneer group of 16 orphans to teach the new novices about goat farming the following year. He also organized self-regulated village groups where the orphans could discuss and manage challenges and share mutual support. Every month all the groups gathered to learn from each other, mostly through discussions of challenges they faced and presentations of solutions. In the groups minutes were kept to document their discussions and decisions.

Erling Krogh, one of the initiators of the project, was working in an action research team at NMBU. In the summer of 2011, he took his colleague and fellow action researcher Sigrid Gjøtterud to Mgeta, primarily to visit the young people who had received the loan of a goat the year before. It was the same story everywhere. Eyes shining with pride, the young dairy farmers stood straight and tall as they described articulately how they cared for their goats and what it meant for them. The change from the despondent, tongue-tied youths Erling had met the previous year was striking. Their strength and self-sufficiency were just as obvious to Sigrid. The visits formed a circle of connection. Sigrid became interested and wanted to get involved. She received funding to start action research on the goat project and joined the group behind Mgeta's Friends.

In 2015, Mgeta's Friends invited a network of trusted friends and donors to take part in a building project. In 2014, the organization had started a major undertaking. In the inner region of Mgeta, secondary school enrolment rates were very low. The obstacles to attendance were greatest for the young girls, who had many household duties and a long walk to school, often up to three hours each way. Many were also sexually assaulted on the way to or from school. Together with the local community, Mgeta's Friends decided to build a hostel for girls next to the school. The school and hostel were located far from good roads and very demanding to build.

So in 2015 Norwegians were allowed to take part in the building project. Thirty-five volunteers from Norway joined the local youth and their families, carrying sand and soil for the casting of bricks, building bunk beds and doing other practical work. Many of the participants described their meeting with the Uluguru mountains, the people and the work on the boarding school as a watershed in their lives. They made their own connections and many become engaged in solidarity projects for Mgeta in their own local communities in Norway.

In 2015, two Norwegian schools, Tokke Primary School in Telemark and the Waldorf school in Moss, Østfold, chose Mgeta and the Uluguru Mountains as their solidarity project. Two teachers from Moss and four from Tokke participated in volunteer work. Pupils at the schools have composed and performed plays in which they compare their own situation with that of pupils in Mgeta, and have made products that they sell at events. In 2017, another trip to Mgeta is planned for teachers and pupils at Norwegian schools wanting to link with a sister school in the Uluguru Mountains.

In ways like this, the connection between the local and the global can also become a connection between two local communities otherwise separated by geography, culture and living conditions. When the global becomes local, it can be easier to form connections. In this example the local community of Mgeta in the Uluguru Mountains is able to form connections to other communities elsewhere on the globe. Seen in this way, there are clear connections between the local community and the wider world, as was illustrated in Figure 3.1.

CHAPTER TWELVE

THE REGIONAL LEARNING SPACE

Over many years' work with local projects connected to natural and cultural resources, it has become apparent that the development of ideas and creativity is boosted when people from different places gather around a common theme. In many cases this involves a linking up of places within a region. A special dynamic then arises in the tension between particular place and common region. The creative boost possibly owes to shared environmental, historical and cultural references combined with individual variations in ways of thinking and in approaching and resolving the real-life issues.

What distinguishes the 'regional'?

Regions accommodate different dimensions than localities do. At the regional level, context and the big picture reveal themselves in ways hidden from view at the local level. This holds for connections in nature, the use of the landscape, and the historical roots and distinctive character and culture of the area. The relationship between the region's resources and the particular ways they are used comes into focus. The identity of people living in a specific geographic location is influenced by the character and uniqueness of the natural and cultural landscape, and is further developed through practical work and social and cultural interaction.

'Region' is a very elastic concept, used in many areas of life, for example in science (climatic regions), politics (administrative units) and the general social realm (the frame of cultural, social and practical everyday life). It is on the last that we shall focus here. A region comprises a number of local communities, which will differ in terms of locality, economic composition, number of inhabitants and so on. And yet these places have some things in common: the main traits of their natural resources, including topography, water and vegetation, and common cultural history, dialect, forms of interaction and other common references that distinguish them from other regions. The geographical size of a region is often no bigger than can be traversed in the course of one's daily activities, be it for work, secondary school, commerce or cultural events. Lorange (1977) interprets the region as 'home ground for people'. In his view it is important that pupils have a conscious perspective of the region they grow up in and that this should be integrated into their education from primary school onwards: 'Study of the region and experience of all its aspects should begin consciously in primary school … In secondary school regional conditions should assume a leading role in teaching' (p. 43).

As a geographical area and locus of cultural identity (territory) for a population, a region is something that is known and part of a common cultural identity. At the same time, it is sufficiently varied and complex to offer new challenges, experiences and learning opportunities. A region will inspire new thinking and innovation within a familiar context. This opens the way to inventive entrepreneurial projects and devising new solutions for familiar problems in the local environment.

When people in different local communities experience the same recurring problems and attempts to solve them, they may find that innovative collaboration at the regional level will offer new angles to approach challenges and solutions. This understanding has underpinned our development and piloting of a course in place-based learning and entrepreneurship in a regional space.

'I found it!' The resources of place

The essence of using place in innovative learning in schools is being able to look at familiar surroundings with new eyes and to imagine what is yet to be. The local community and region are full of exciting resources for those who have the eye to see them.

What is a 'resource' and how do we identify it? Nothing is a resource in itself, neither in culture nor in nature. Something becomes a resource when someone discovers its usefulness for some purpose – which depends on that person's ability to *imagine* what this purpose might be. In other words, mapping resources involves connecting to the future and picturing what is possible, what is the desired outcome and how to achieve it. The ability to do this is one of the characteristics of an entrepreneur. Who better than the Ash Lad can shed light on the matter? For the Ash Lad, learning means looking at oneself and one's surroundings with new eyes. So how can schools, through local curricula, help pupils to find their inner Ash Lad?

> The school must develop their urge to get going and keep going. It must spur their will to persevere and develop their energy to resist loss of nerve and overcome their own inner resistance and vacillation.' (NCC 1997, p. 5)

What did the Ash Lad see?

The fairy tale journey is often described as a long and perilous road, writes Sundland (1995, p. 57) in *Det var en gang et menneske* [Once upon a Time a Human]. Reaching the goal is not inevitable. The storyteller often emphasizes the toil, the perseverance, the protagonist's refusal to give up no matter what the odds. In Norwegian tales we see the landscape depicted: endless forests, steep mountains, wide open spaces, rivers, fjords, lakes, on and on to the open sea. There is no mention of highways, only secret ways that no one has walked before, the self-chosen path, our personal way in life, perhaps.

The Ash Lad is not just a person, but a quality inside us. The castle is not just a building but 'a dream of spiritual richness and purity' (ibid., p. 27). In

'The Seven Foals' by Asbjørnsen and Moe (2009) we read, 'When they had travelled a long, long way, the foal asked, "Do you see anything?" "No", said the Ash Lad. So they continued a good while. "What about now?", the foal asked. "Do you see anything now?" "No, nothing", said the boy. So they travelled on for many, many miles, over hill and dale. "Now, then?", the foal asked. "Do you see anything now?" "Yes", said the Ash Lad. "Now I can see what looks like a strip of blue, far, far away." "Yes", said the foal. "That's a river we've got to cross."'

If you want to contribute to and engage with the world, you must see it in your mind's eye first. Hence the story's recurring question: 'Do you see anything yet?' The Ash Lad is he who undergoes trials and overcomes them. His spiritual energy is enough to overcome even the greatest exhaustion and temptation. And then a transformation may occur, a new vision may appear within him. The Ash Lad has the capacity to generate inner pictures; he uses his imagination and believes what he sees. He's seen the golden castle shining before him on the horizon, and set out to reach it, thereby committing himself to the future. He perceives the full value of everything, no matter how small and awkward it may appear at first sight. Who would believe that an old shoe sole, a pottery fragment or a dead magpie could come in useful? It is thanks to his creative vision and motivation that Espen the Ash Lad can see the worth that has passed everyone else by.

The Ash Lad chooses freedom and serendipity; he goes it alone yet connects with others and everything that lives. Through inner growth, anchoring and belonging, we too can summon this power and capacity. We can connect to our environment and draw on our own values in creative work, just like the Ash Lad.

The story of RMT is a vivid example of how a pedagogical and social programme can be developed in intimate dialogue with place and its specific resources and layers of stories.

Exploring the encounter with the material

Jorunn Barane

I visited Ruskin Mill College for the first time in 2007, when researching my master's thesis, which was titled 'The Place, the Dialogue and the Story' (Barane 2007). I was told that I should stay for at least one week in order to get a true impression of the place. Since then I have visited the college every year, either with study groups or with students. In November 2015, I returned yet again as part of a pilot-project collaboration between NMBU and SJH. I took part in three different workshops, having in mind some predefined questions:

- What does the material demand from me?
- What emotions does it evoke in me?
- What does it give back to me?

In addition, I interviewed students and teachers during the working sessions and breaks. In doing so, I sought to understand how students learn through dialogue, and work with various materials in craft-based learning.

Pottery and clay workshop in Stroud

> The most difficult thing is the decision to act, the rest is merely tenacity. The fears are paper tigers. You can do anything you decide to do. You can act to change and control your life; and the procedure, the process is its own reward. (Amelia Earhart)[9]

'Lansdown Pottery, Centre for Science and Art', says the blue sign above the door. I will be spending the day here working with Sam, a teacher and ceramist, and his class. It is rather intimidating to step into his workshop, to build relations both with new people and the new material, which is clay. It seems that the biggest step is having the will to open the door and enter.

Once inside, I meet Sam and a student. They are in the middle of examining and discussing the student's work: dog and cat bowls in different sizes and shapes, kiln fired and glazed. The task is now to choose the piece that the student likes the most – the one with the best shape and design, which he can reproduce in a series to sell at the Christmas market. The teacher tells him that this really is a challenge – to pick one and go for it! The student picks a bowl with a well-balanced, upright form; I can see he has chosen the right one.

Then Sam begins to tell me about the clay the same way he does with all his students, starting with where it comes from, how it is made, the geological processes, the ice ages, the minerals pressed together and refined over the millennia. Sam is from Uganda and has worked with clay since he was a little boy. He has built houses from this material. We have to start at the beginning, he says. This is important. Sam's students must go out and literally dig out the clay from the valley. We have to experience the connectedness of things, a major challenge today, when we usually see only fragments of processes. We have to start at the beginning and experience the whole chain of connections, to be in context and create relationships in the world. This is what the students need.

After the students have dug out the clay, they learn to know the material and how to use it. They take a lump and squeeze it in their hands, stir in water and work it until they find the right consistency. Then comes the process of shaping the clay into a form. When it is fired, a completely new chemical compound forms, ready for glazing and patterns and colour.

Before students are allowed to use the potter's wheel, they need to learn other techniques, starting with coils. We roll out long sausages and lay them in a circle. I shape a jar form, working in silence till I get stuck. I let it rest and start something else. Sam shows me the rolling pin method; rolling out the base and then the sides, joining them together with watered-down clay. I hit a dead end, not knowing where my piece is heading, what it is becoming. I take a break and come back to see something completely new, from another angle – and can start working again. It's up to me to decide, in collaboration with the material and the tutor. I suddenly see that this is going to become a jug. I make the spout and try different tools for polishing, jointing and smoothing. The jug is steady and solid. Sam helps me with the handle (Figure 12.1).

Figure 12.1. Tutor Sam Makumbe; Jorunn's jug; cups and bowls in Lucy's workshop.

The teacher demonstrates how to make consistent forms and straight edges. I can say straight away that I like the coil method best, because it feels closest to me. My neighbour has managed to make a bowl on the wheel. We clap and congratulate him. He is very proud.

Turning green wood in Horsley

It is a moist and mild November morning in the beech woods surrounding Ruskin Mill College. We gather tools in the shed: saw, axe and wedges. Richard Turley, our teacher, explains why they felled the trees yesterday. They were standing too close together, very tall and thin. A sudden gale could have knocked them down, potentially causing damage. Removing some trees gives the rest more space to grow and develop their canopies – and their roots, improving their stability.

Leaves in a variety of colours cover the steep hillside, imparting the warm atmosphere that is the signature of beech woods. For the students it is a challenge to keep their footing, let alone to carry tools and logs on their shoulders. They won't learn to use the chainsaw until the third year. We examine the tree lying in front of us and discuss how to cut correct lengths and avoid pinching the hand saw. We slide blocks under the trunk to raise it off the ground and set to work with the two-man saw. Hand sawing requires physical strength and a person on either side of the trunk. We have to find a common rhythm and lead the saw precisely. It is an intimate task, needing tacit communication, and will.

You have to prepare the students. It can take some time to ready the will to act, so that they can start to relate to the task at hand. We are slowly getting warmer. We place the log upright, take the wedge away and study the position of the knots. This is green wood, and we can hear the sound of the fibres tearing as the split extends down the length of the log. We divide it into four equal parts and carry them back to the workshop. Now the teacher draws a circle at each end of the pieces; we are going to make rolling pins. I am given a drawknife to shave off the edges in long movements; the wood feels like butter. When the rounding is complete, we mount our workpieces on the lathe. Then it's time to sharpen our tools (Figure 12.2).

Figure 12.2. Richard Turley, green woodwork tutor, demonstrates how the simple lathe works.

Now the challenge begins. While my foot treads the pedal to make the workpiece rotate back and forth, my hands manipulate the chisel to plane the wood smooth. The damp November weather has made my muscles stiff; coordination is difficult. The resistance in myself and the material is beginning to surface. Now I need the will to continue, to be accurate, to hold the chisel exactly perpendicular to the surface of the wood without gouging it. After a while I need help. I am not able to do this task at the first attempt.

The next day I get another chance. I have better coordination of arms and legs, better concentration. I shape handles at both ends, a little rounded so they sit well in the hand. I still need some help with the rounding – and getting the rolling pin smooth – but I don't give up till the work is complete. The result looks good! I show it to others and get responses; now we can talk about baking and new recipes. Many are impressed and want to know how I made it. The new rolling pin affords conversations, new ideas, laughter and life, empowering and energizing. With its help I can communicate with others in new ways. From felling the tree to finished product, the whole process has been performed in a short time. The rolling pin rests in my hands, shining. I am proud and can see others becoming inspired. I get to meet new people who are happy to chat; the process from tree to rolling pin is something everyone can understand (Figure 12.3).

Figure 12.3. Finished rolling pin from green wood, made in one-and-a-half days – the process from chopping down the tree to sawing, splitting, rounding and turning.

During a break, I talk with 'Alex', age 17, from Swindon, who is chopping and stacking wood. Yes, he likes it here, he tells me. Especially being out in the woods. He has been here for two years. His hometown is dangerous, he says. Wherever he walks, he has to look over his shoulder. The neighbourhood he grew up in is notorious for stabbings and drugs; he's always scared there. At the college he feels safe. He enjoys practical work: 'I have a talent for it.'

Another boy, 'Tom', 17, was meant to be at the wood workshop today but is not feeling well. He can't bring himself to do the work, even though he is happy to be here, gets on well with his teacher and knows he is capable of working with the material. Tom has already made the components of a beautiful stool; all he has left to do is fit the legs to the seat. On the seat he has engraved a large heart. The stool is a present for his family. However, this weekend he's going to visit his mother, who is a drug addict. She has told him that his father is dead and that he will never see him again. For a long time, Tom has wanted to meet his family. Nothing remains of his father, he's been told, not even a photograph. Both his brothers are in prison, convicted for stabbing. When the woodwork teacher first introduced him to the tools, he knew them from his childhood, from all the fighting going on. After returning from a weekend with his family, Tom is very confused; he is unable to concentrate and needs to see his therapist. It's no consolation that the teacher promises that after lunch he can make a fire in the woods, which is one of his favourite activities.

Metalwork in Sheffield

In the 10th century, a castle was built at the confluence of the River Sheaf and River Don to control trade. Around this castle the town slowly grew. By the fourteenth century, it was known for its knife production. Two centuries later it was the biggest manufacturer of cutlery in England. New methods for steel production and silver plating were developed here, and during the industrial revolution Sheffield experienced enormous growth in wealth and population.

We find our way through the city to Freeman College, impressed by the richness of architecture from different periods, derelict industrial buildings and all the sounds and smells. We see long rows of workers' houses and new art installations with running water. The college is housed in a former metal factory. We can see the old machines that were used to produce cutlery in the workshop. There is a smell of oil and dust. The windows are placed high up on the walls, so we cannot look out. This feels like a masculine workplace.

Our tutor Matt has arranged everything for the workshop we are going to take part in. He has punched out circular pieces of copper and pewter in different sizes. We are told to dress in aprons and safety shoes, and Matt introduces us to the tools and working processes. Then we set to work. After a while, I stop hammering a piece of pewter and ask myself, 'What do I really want from this material?' This is the first step in the student's learning process: to be mindful of the transformation that is about to begin. What I want to make, the shape of it, its function – such considerations lead the eye to the tools at hand, each of them able to shape the material in their individual way.

The next thing I learn from the tutor is to tap in small circles, seven times, and then pause, doing this repeatedly in rhythmical series. We try out different working surfaces and tools. The pewter is flexible and easily shaped. The flat metal disc starts to become a bowl. After a while, I ask it, 'What is your intention to be, in response to my hammering?' The question opens a new dialogue with the material. Perhaps it wants to be a brooch. But how to make that form?

During the break we discuss the metals and their provenance, placing them in a story from the Neolithic and the rise of metallurgy, to our present technological age. We imagine how this might develop into a greater cultural narrative, weaving in the location and mining of ores and the trade routes they passed along.

Student work is on display at the college. Gleaming copper platters spun on a lathe, silver vases and cutlery, Christmas decorations cast in pewter. Not to forget garden tools made in bronze with wooden shafts. The students guide us around their workshop. One student is making a neat little snake in silver. He's absorbed in his work but very proud to show it to us. Another is working on a wolf with blue stone eyes, which he will wear around his neck as an amulet. It's as if, intuitively, the students have some kind of access to the old wisdom related to these animals and hope for their protection in their challenging lives (Figure 12.4).

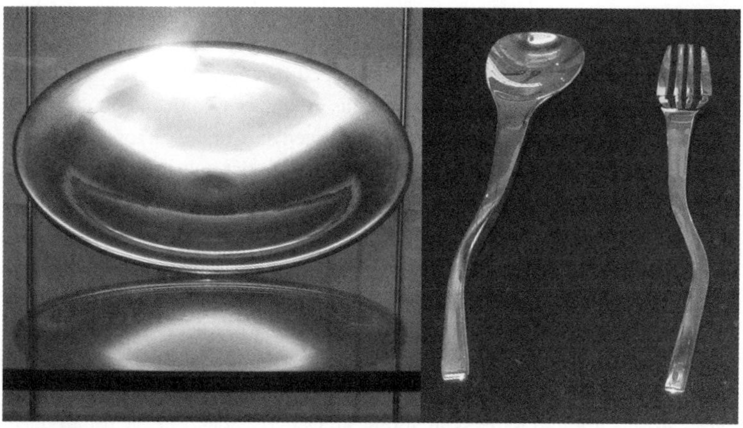

Figure 12.4. Work by students at Freeman College: Hammered copper bowl and novel spoon and fork designs in silver.

I return to my own work and assemble the pewter and copper pieces I have hammered into shape. I make a hole in the middle of both and join them together with a brass spiral. Then I make two holes for a leather cord so it can be a necklace. My storyteller's ornament is ready for use.

What does the material demand from me? What emotions does it evoke? And what do I get back from it? From making the brooch I learnt that you are limited by the time available. The glow in the copper surprised me, giving me new energy on a cold and dark November day. This would have been a familiar situation a hundred years ago, before electricity became widely available. In those days, people took out their silver cutlery and copper plates, and polished them so they would glow in the dark times of the year. As a storyteller, one can give voice to the gleaming metal hidden in the mountain with the help of local myths and legends. Such stories can also bring energy and light to people. The brooch tells a twofold story: how what my hands create leaves traces sourced deep in my own biography and braided with the imprint of the place – the unique site – where it is made (see Figure 12.5).

Figure 12.5. Jorunn's storyteller brooch in pewter copper and brass and garden trowels.

Transformation through resistance and encounter with material

When you turn a clay bowl or make a rolling pin from green wood, you leave something of yourself in the final product. The shape of the jug made by my hands reveals something of my inner self. Part of your inner life is exposed to the world when you bring your products to market. This is a form of intimate communication that allows others to respond. The communication is indirect, through the material, but it is very personal nonetheless. It may even have a price attached to it. This can be a helpful to those who struggle with relating to other people.

In these ways, students at Ruskin Mill are helped to see their potential and to appreciate their knowledge and competence. When you value yourself, your uniqueness and value will be manifest to others. In the encounter between seller and customer, something special can occur: respect for, and understanding of, the process you have gone through.

In the meeting between student and place, both parties are transformed. The genius of place and the individuality of the student come together. This is a repetitive, creative process in which new beginnings and opportunities are continually generated. At Ruskin Mill they call it 'reimagining potential', which is always embodied in the material, the place and the individual human being. For the student it is primarily a process of finding the right theme or material by testing several during their first term at the college. Then comes the work of developing enough will and strength to release the potential latent in oneself and the material. For young people this is a matter of identity and communication – of exposing their personality to the world.

The challenge lies in stepping up to face the resistance in the material and ourselves, and summoning the patience, energy and will to transform both. Through resistance we experience ourselves and our potential. This allows us to develop our capacity to reimagine our relations with other people and our surroundings.

CHAPTER THIRTEEN

LEARNING AS A PROCESS OF CHANGE

For young people growing up today, the global ecological changes now underway have existential significance. They are hard to ignore or forget, given the media coverage of global warming and the effects of climate change we encounter in our daily lives. As well as changing our lifestyles and behaviour, we must change how we make plans. We must learn to understand how little we really know about the future, which is not simply an extension of how things are now, or how they have come to be. We assume that science and education can equip us to master the future through planning, but more and more often we are exposed to unpredictable events that place stress on nature and human society alike. A major consequence of climate change is that large groups of people are being forced to migrate from their homes in order to survive. This creates new challenges and conflicts.

The notion of 'unknown unknowns' has been used in recent years to describe what 'we don't know we don't know' (Selman 2012) and provides a vivid summation of how vulnerable we are in the face of environmental challenges. The more uncertain we are, the more important it is to learn from our experiences and to be able to cope with change. These are fundamentals that should be practised in schools as a matter of course.

Our traditional way of community planning proceeds from specific, often quantifiable goals for what we seek to achieve in the short and long term. At the same time, experience tells us that such goals are rarely attained, simply because conditions change in unforeseeable ways. Drawing on climate and environmental research, people in diverse disciplines and research communities have recognized that planning in complex natural and human-influenced environments (places, cultural landscapes – 'social-ecological systems') must, besides building on acquired knowledge, be able to learn through experience and adapt to changing conditions. The latter quality, *resilience*, can be applied to a landscape's capacity to retain its distinctive character and fundamental structures and functions when subjected to stresses such as floods, storms, drought, etc. The key to this capacity is the landscape's ability to learn from unusual events and to 'remember' its learning (Pleininger and Bieling 2012).

If we consider such challenges from the perspective of local communities, we can see how important it is to connect basic human values and educational goals with creative spirit, envisioning processes, and activities rooted in their setting. We must strengthen our attachment to our place and not let negative messages tip us into paralysis and apathy. It is easy to fall into habits that disconnect us from ourselves as creative forces in the weave of life, so it is vital that we establish good relationships with place. Here, schools fulfil an important function as rehearsal spaces. When this is integrated into the community it can become sustainable entrepreneurship – or 'ecopreneurship'.

On poetry and truth

> Education shall impart in the learner a zest for life, the courage to tackle it, and a desire to use and extend what they learn. Children, when they begin their schooling, embark upon a great adventure which, with luck and care, can last them a lifetime. (NCC 1997, p. 5)

Dahlin (2004, p. 16) observes how we have disenchanted the world and attach importance only to what we can know for sure, to facts and information. We are fixated on external reality, the physical world. Scientific knowledge has high status and is often perceived as certain and objective. The 'inner' world tends to be silenced. How can we poetize the world and awaken its many unseen facets? Is it possible to fantasize and create truthfully? How do we present the truth, and what is truth? Does it exist outwardly as facts or in what a person experiences? Is not all acknowledgement of truth an inner recognition that something meshes on an emotional level?

The storyteller often wishes to wake an *experience of truth* in the listener. The experience of truth is dependent on one recognizing it on an emotional level. Therefore, it is important that a narrative not only makes clear what is happening on the external plane, but also refers to what is happening inwardly in reactions, feelings and thoughts. To stir recognition, one must set aside neutrality and dare to embellish and interpret. When we tell a story, we must dare to add our own emotions, experiences and values. Stories are often about people or beings who have to make choices, risk something, win or lose. We cannot confine ourselves to describing what is happening as events on a concrete plane. When we tell a story we must depict the inner process, for it is here that the real action takes place (Svarstad 2012). The same applies when we are speaking of the living world. In this alternation between being immersed in participation and standing apart to see a thing from outside, new recognition dawns.

To be experienced as true, a story must be owned by its teller. This means leaving out what obscures and obstructs the telling, and adding to clarify the important things, as Astrup does when he depicts the nature of Western Norway. Colour is needed to inspire the listeners and lead them deeper into the story. When you are telling a story and creating art in the moment, you have to engage your other brain hemisphere, the home of imagination and creativity. For it is poetry's duty to go ahead and make sure that truth is seen and well received, as in the following story.

How truth came to wear clothes

A long time ago Truth wandered among humankind. Truth was old, thin and as naked as the day she was born. Wherever she went, people averted their heads, wanting nothing to do with her. One morning late in autumn, when the weather was wet and grey, Truth went into town. She was miserable.

The raw cold cut through her bare skin. She felt tired, sad and hungry as she walked. If only she were not so lonely! If only the townsfolk would acknowledge her! Arriving at the town square, she saw that a big crowd had gathered: young and old pressed together, listening to someone speak. Curious, Truth approached them. As she got closer she heard a familiar voice. Who should it be but Poetry standing there! Now Poetry was just as old as she, but unlike Truth he did not go about naked. On the contrary, he wore an extremely elegant outfit: his tall, strong figure was clothed in garments of the most beautiful colours and fabrics, from softest wool to lustrous velvet and silk. His face was ageless. That's not to say that he didn't look his years, but his eyes were so intense and bright and his voice so warm and expressive. 'How beautiful he is', thought Truth. She bowed her head and felt close to weeping. She looked down at her body, her shrunken limbs and wrinkled skin. Where had all ease and well-being gone? Why was it that by living so long, Truth was just shrivelling up? She turned, wanting to be alone, to get away.

Then she heard footsteps behind her and a voice saying, 'Well I never, is that really you?' Truth looked up and met the kindly eyes of Poetry. 'How are you?', he asked.

'Not well', she replied. 'I am shunned. That's old age for you – being left to fend for oneself.'

Poetry looked at her gravely. 'No, my dear. It's not your age; it's because you are naked. People don't know what to make of candour. They can only accept a thing if it is wrapped and prettied up a bit. Look at me! I'm so popular, it's almost too much. And why am I popular, might you ask? It's because I never show myself in the nude, that's why.' When Truth said nothing he continued, 'Allow me to invite you to my home. There you can take a steaming hot bath with aromatic oils and pick some clothes from my collection. And when you are dressed and in good spirits, I'd like us to take a trip to town together. You'll see a big difference.'

Truth was about to say no, but she hesitated. Why not give it a try? Perhaps accepting help is not so bad, and, besides, there was nothing to lose. So she changed her mind and accepted the invitation.

Poetry had a huge loft of a dressing room. Its walls were lined from floor to ceiling with wardrobes filled with garments for every occasion, whim or mood. After many hours of trying on outfits and scrutinizing in front of the mirror, a choice was finally made: a long, gracefully draped gown in the most resplendent colours.

'Well, I declare!', said Poetry, 'That's more like it.'

Truth looked at her reflection and was delighted to see roses in her cheeks and a sparkle in her eyes. And yes, she had to admit, she didn't look half bad. Elegantly, Poetry offered his arm. And so they went into town together that autumn evening. And the strange thing was that events unfolded precisely as Poetry had foretold. The townsfolk flocked to them. They addressed Truth eagerly, warmly, curiously and attentively. And not only that, many even invited her to dine at their homes! From that evening on, the two were inseparable: Poetry and Truth, ever arm in arm. People looked up to them and approached them wherever they went.

'It's strange to think', said Poetry as they headed home one evening, 'that before I met you I was pure fantasy.'

'And you've made me alive again', answered Truth, smiling up at him.

'In our meeting we've become something bigger than our individual selves,' continued Poetry. 'We've become a story.'

'That's what we are!', concluded Truth, sounding pleased and surprised. And both of them knew that deep down in the bottom of their hearts they were one, because they completed one another in every way.

(Yiddish tale from the 12th century, adapted after Marianne Svarstad [2012].)

Principles for transformative learning

Landscape's capacity to frame ecological and social resilience has its counterpoint in a form of learning that emphasizes inner change and creativity. We find such an emphasis in the principles of transformative learning. The first principle of transformative learning is *purposeful and heuristic learning*, in which learners together ask questions, establish goals and find ways to attain them. The second principle is about *confronting power and engaging difference*. The third involves *testing one's limits*, as learning often occurs when learners come up against resistance, experience something unfamiliar or face challenges that prompt innovation. Next comes *reflection* by learners about their experience of themselves, others and society. The last principle is the adult's *function of modelling*, that is, the teacher or instructor as a good example for their students (Illeris 2013, p. 28).

Transformative learning turns on individual experience and fostering critical reflection, and also a dialogue involving its participants' attitudes, emotions, personalities and values. Emphasis is also placed on a holistic orientation, including emotional and social dimensions as well as the cognitive dimension. Based on his own and others' research, Edward W. Taylor (2008) argues that abstract knowledge is too dominant over other modes of learning. To transform our self-understanding, we need to include deeper modes of participatory learning that involve feeling, will and body. Transformative learning theory is therefore critical to the simple belief that knowledge alone can be an agent of change.Often a resistance has to be overcome, which creates community. Participants develop and tell stories, engage in cooperative enquiry and express themselves physically. Taylor believes that transformative learning primarily rests on learner-based teaching in which teachers function as initiators and facilitators. Decisions and evaluations are made in common (Illeris 2013, p. 26). Let's now look at an example of learning as a creative process.

Sawing wood in Class 9. Photograph: SJH

Splitting wood. Photograph: SJH.

Baking pizza. Photograph: SJH.

Entrepreneurship in Class 6: from wood to pizza

One winter, Class 6 made regular outings to nearby woodlands to cut and store firewood. The learning objectives included, among other things, the handling of axe and saw when felling trees, and splitting and stacking wood. Come the spring and milder weather, the pupils wanted to make pizza in our wood-fired ovens. Class 6 had food and health on the timetable, so now half the group were firing up the ovens with wood they had cut themselves, while the others were in the school kitchen making pizza dough and tomato sauce. When the ovens had reached the right temperature after about two hours of firing, the embers were scraped out and the pupils baked pizzas in the Italian style. They had never tasted better! A boy promptly suggested that the class build an oven in the school yard. He thought they could earn good money by selling pizza on Friday afternoons to weary parents who would appreciate a ready meal after a long working week.

Seeing what is not yet there

To plan such a task, it is necessary to picture the steps and activity through the winter months and link learning objectives to subject, skills and attitudes. As a teacher you can formulate the pathway together with your pupils, and then they can help to evaluate it in the spring. The starting point is an activity, and that the learning will occur in a concrete place. From activity and place new ideas can then emerge, as when the boy suddenly perceives the economics of selling pizza to tired parents on Fridays after school. Here he is demonstrating advanced, compound thinking. His statement combines a number of different experiences that, having passed through senses, emotions and facts, are assembled and expressed as a new idea. He has acquired an overview, tested and made new choices, to reveal a new connection, something he has not seen before. He has combined things in a new way and thereby reached new insight. The concept of competence thus involves the ability to employ the capacities one has acquired in relevant situations (Krogh 2010).

The key is to have a holistic plan before starting an activity. It is helpful if the pupils can contribute to laying the learning path and finding the right questions. Children have abundant imagination, and involving them in the planning gives them the chance to train their imaginative skills, since devising integrated outdoor learning tasks requires imagination. One has to think through all that may or may not occur.

The experiences along the way and in the process stand in focus. But sometimes one has to change course because of the weather or other unanticipated events. No matter how thorough the preparation, there will always be challenges along the way. We only have to think of the mountains as a learning space in late autumn. It is essential to practise observing and understanding the interplay of the sometimes inhospitable forces of nature. Teachers are quick to call off a hike after seeing the weather forecast on their smartphone, but what signals does this send to the pupils?

In his book *The Beautiful Risk of Education*, Gert Biesta (2013) makes the point that in matters of evolving, maturing and becoming as human beings we cannot avoid risk.

Education that strives to become a well-oiled, risk-free system – what he calls 'strong education' – destroys its own foundations. 'This is why the risk of education – what I tend to call the beautiful risk of education – is so very important' (p. 146).

Biesta uses the term 'beautiful risk' to describe the risk that is integral to daring – we must learn to dare. He finds support in John Dewey's (2005) alternative to the idea of linguistic communication as transmission of readymade meaning from one individual to another. As storytellers we must also share something of ourself, show who we are, be vulnerable to the risk of daring. In *vulnerable education* it's all about venturing on to the dance floor or plunging in the river. Without resistance and the need to overcome it, it makes no sense to speak of transformative learning. There is a close connection between the risks that artists lay themselves open to – all that they don't yet know or haven't yet seen or done – and innovation. Biesta shows in his book how openness and vulnerability in the process underpins all human growth, and that living with the undetermined and uncertain is inextricably linked to creativity. For education and teachers this means daring to open up their process – 'a process that is not only radically open and undetermined, but also generative and creative' (Biesta 2013, p. 35).

Here we are back with the Ash Lad – the way is the goal in itself. If school and pupils are to learn how to face the future, they must venture into the uncertainty in the tension between tradition and innovation. The suggestion to build a wood-burning oven at the school farm, in order to raise money for school trips by baking pizza for parents on Fridays, is such a venture. Thinking it, saying it and doing it take guts. If we look a little deeper at this example, we will also find that the boy's creativity and boldness did not come from thin air.

Dewey (2005) is interested in the continuity in aesthetic experience from sensation (intake from the environment), to inner movement (emotion), to what we obtain from ideas and the world of concrete expression. It is the taste itself which gives a 'taste for more'. This example, in Dewey's terms, is an experience so deeply aesthetic, so moving, that a sensation (an emotion) sets thought and will in motion.

How to develop work across subjects and get experts to join us in the field to organize and practise transformation? With good sense and judgement, we would then be able to set sail for unknown waters and take risks – and there's no shame in turning back, as Norwegian trekkers say. Teachers cannot bear this responsibility alone, so it is necessary to turn to local professionals who have the relevant expertise. In Africa they say it takes a community to raise a child. Teachers cannot be expected to bear this responsibility and risk alone. Only jointly, as teachers, parents, school, professionals and local authority, can we safely lead this risky process of education. Learning is found in pushing ourselves further than we believed we could go, testing our limits, for example by spending the night in the open by a campfire and studying the starry sky. We must step out of our comfort zone, challenge ourselves and venture into the unknown, into the river, into risk. But at this moment the group must hold together. Here there's a chance to practise innovation on an outer level and transformation on an inner level, to overcome our limits and extend our boundaries.

CHAPTER FOURTEEN

GROWING PEOPLE, GROWING PLACE

Transformative learning centres on a developmental process in which people become more than they were; we grow by taking part in processes that offer us experience and reflection, resistance and challenges, cooperation and collaboration. However, we have seen that learning as a process of change and creativity can involve an extra dimension: the encounter with space and place, with materiality, and through it the senses. Here the will gains purchase. The world makes its presence felt, giving the self something to connect to, to grow in and out of. It is through the resistance in material that transformation can occur. We must dare to be challenged physically and emotionally in order to surmount resistance – find solutions, improvise on the spot. From this perspective, theories of ecopreneurship can widen the perspective of transformative learning to include processes on both sides of the transformation.

This eye for nature, place and the world – for the understanding of processes and the ability to intervene meaningfully to address problems experienced in one's local environment – ecopreneurship shares all this in common with *education for sustainable development*. Then again, what we have presented here in some depth – the connection to the deeper intellectual and spiritual processes in a person – is often treated more superficially in learning materials about sustainable development (Tilbury 2002). The one perspective focuses on inner processes and the self; growing people. The other focuses on the outer processes; growing places. The red thread of our story has attempted to balance and join these viewpoints into an integrated perspective. To cultivate the whole human being we must open our eyes to *how* a person's inner life is creatively reaching out to the world, and *how* the outside world is reaching in.

It's likewise possible to see an affinity between the concepts of *entrepreneurship* and *ecopreneurship*, given the former's emphasis that growing up and education are about developing the ability to create something that is yet to be. But again our narrative has opened this concept beyond narrow business connotations to include social and ecological dimensions.

The school's double mission

Using place in innovative learning in schools means looking at familiar surroundings with new eyes and imagining what is yet to be. The local community and region are full of exciting resources for those who have the eyes to see them! This is one of the characteristics of an entrepreneur. Who better than the Ash Lad can shed light on the

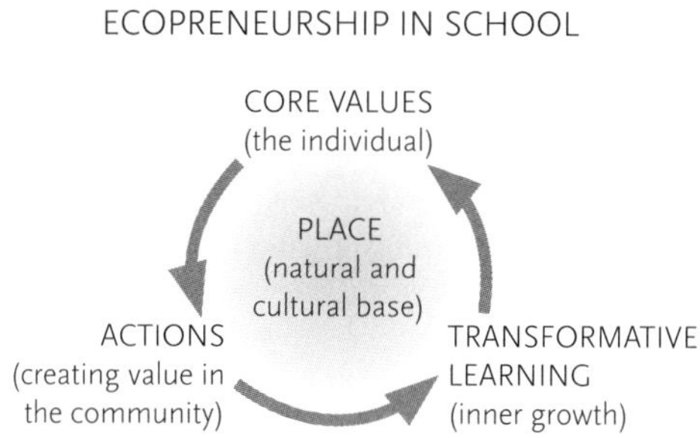

Figure 14.1. Values-based actions that start from place form the basis for both outer value creation and pupils' inner growth.

matter? For the Ash Lad, learning means looking at oneself and one's surroundings with new eyes. So how can schools, through local curricula, help pupils to find their inner Ash Lad?

To develop future-minded learning, schools need to change. Such change will occur in contact with the community, and not through abstract curricular processes. The connecting thought in our narrative has been that place and learning, after a lengthy separation, are reconnecting to form *a new core of values* for schools to build on. We live at a time when schools and all those who work in and around them face a double mission. The first mission has to do with the individual and with inner development. The second hinges on the place, environment and local community the school is part of. The change that schools will need to undergo is clear: they have to understand why these two missions can no longer be held apart and consider what the implications of this are.

Ecopreneurship in education

Ecopreneurship in education (Figure 14.1), as we understand it, involves changing both *intention* and the school's *ability to translate* its intention into pedagogical theory and practice. The Aurland model – with its experience of how learning can grow as an inner and outer process, in circles from nearby to the entire region – is just one example of how such change can be enacted. The methodological and theoretical tools we introduce in this book are similarly only examples and fragments of such theory. The interesting thing is that we cannot formulate theories within existing disciplinary boundaries, since pedagogy and learning theory, and theory on placemaking and development of place, at present belong to separate academic disciplines. It's a similar story in the field of practice: in a municipality or a region, those who work in care, health or education operate in their own sealed-off environments and departments, separate from those who work in place development, the local environment, nature and public administration in the local community. Connecting them may be a task for the future, just as it will be a task to connect thinking from the two different disciplines to form new, silo-breaking theory of practice for a renewed school within a renewed local democracy – where the renewal of natural and cultural heritage will also play its part.

Our concept of ecopreneurship entwines the development of people and the development of their surroundings. We therefore need insights and methods that can connect and comprehend both the ecology, transformation and development of people, and the development of place.

CHAPTER FIFTEEN

A MODEL FOR INTEGRATED COMMUNITY DEVELOPMENT

In this final chapter we offer examples of how to go about developing place-based projects that write themselves into the story of a place, locally and regionally. To summarize briefly: we have used local curriculum work as a tool to join together goals or value dimensions that in schools are normally divided. This is, first, a divide that schools themselves struggle with: a rift between curriculum goals and the core curriculum, between those who prioritize learning outcomes and those who are interested in educating pupils. Places, tasks, resources and undertakings that are located not inside the school walls but beyond them can be used to bridge this rift. Second, there is a divide between the educational mission of schools and their duty to help tackle today's ecological and social crises. This is something that local curriculum work can address.

Here we are dealing with four different dimensions (see Figure 15.1): the development of pupils and place (1, 2), and the innovative capacity of the school and the local community (3, 4). Let's look at some methodological aspects of this matrix which feature in local curriculum work.

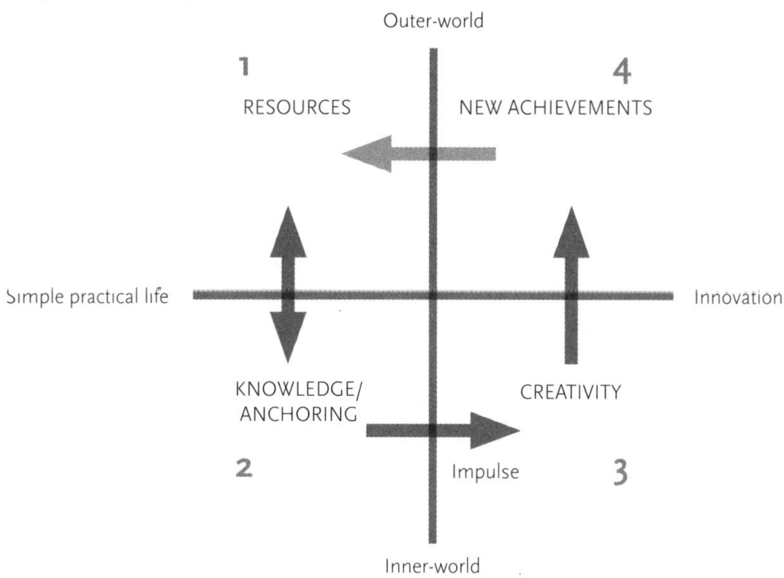

Figure 15.1. Simplified version of Geddes's model, based on Defries (1927) and Welter (2002).

Four phases and dimensions of innovative learning

The entrepreneur or innovator is able to bring something new to life, something that alters established practice as it occurs in a place, either socially or culturally or physically (Haukeland 2010). Place-based 'entrepreneurship', as we use the term, means spotting opportunities and acting as a constructive and creative innovator in a local setting and landscape. Entrepreneurship may seem to be about major enterprises and large-scale initiatives. It can be, of course. But it can also be about small, often inconspicuous initiatives sneaking into the world. In time, these small steps from idea to realization leave their mark on a place, making it special and unlike other places.

Is it possible to clarify in an integrated model the connections between learning processes, development of place and the role that schools play in future-minded entrepreneurship? When we were preparing and implementing the regional course in place-based entrepreneurship and learning, we took inspiration from Patrick Geddes.

Geddes's life's work included, among other things, pioneering work in planning how to develop a region's potentials through identifying and enhancing landscape characteristics, natural resources and cultural and entrepreneurial competences (Lorange 1977). Both in his lifetime and after, Geddes has been a controversial figure. Many were challenged by his unconventional and intuitive approach and his facility for interdisciplinary and holistic thinking. Yet he has had a profound influence on a number of areas, including urban planning, regional development, sociology and pedagogy (Boardman 1978).

Geddes's models for place development and learning in a regional context have found resonance throughout the world, and in recent years have been reinvigorated in landscape-scale planning and management and also education under names such as 'bioregional planning' and 'landscape urbanism'.

Our model starts from the assumption that learning happens on both an external plane (out-world) and an inner plane (in-world), in the tension between practical daily life and creative innovation. The learning processes that arise in the varying conditions of the place (its nature, culture and human resources), in place identity and in mastery tied to personal experiences form the basis for innovation and entrepreneurship in a regional context. The regional perspective is pivotal to forming robust connections and enterprises that build on the resource base of the place – what we today call 'sustainable value creation'. The main principles presented in Figure 15.1 may be explained as follows.

1. Field 1 contains the everyday life we live as individuals and members of a populace ('folk') connected to a place. Place and community have a character and an individuality formed by natural conditions in interplay with agriculture, industry, commerce, building and all the other activities the populace engages in. With respect to

the school's role as a change agent this field has to do with our local and regional surroundings. The is accessible to both teachers and pupils. It is a common space and our shared responsibility.

2. Field 2 concerns the 'in-world', that is, what each individual perceives and feels about the place. It involves the activities, skills and knowledge that the individual has attached to the place and that may be expressed through notions like 'place identity' and 'belonging'. With respect to the school's role as a development actor, this field is about resource persons and the knowledge that can be accessed through partnering with local businesses and institutions. It is again a common space, and both teachers and pupils can learn from it.

   There is a looping interplay between fields 1 and 2 as long as the activity pattern and relationship remain fundamentally stable. One becomes better at understanding and honing skills to master what one already knows. Identity remains constant. In terms of this book's aim to lay a methodological foundation for value-based knowledge development and learning to contribute to sustainable place development, real learning will necessitate a break with established and familiar patterns.

   Whether it be baking flatbread or apple pressing, we have found an inbuilt impulse that is crucial, able to shift perspective from the status quo to a genuine sense of future possibilities. In some cases, inner images of the future situation may also be formed. In our schematic model the question is how to move from the left-hand side – field 2 – across to field 3.

3. Learning through place-based work strengthens the identity of place, gives an active sense of mastery and facilitates the seeking of new possibilities for the future. In a learning context this will be the springboard for a self-generated process of learning and mastery of new skills. Only one path leads from this phase of inner vision: the path of seeking to realize the vision. Again, this opens up a space for new ideas about what the school can do locally to develop learning arenas, and about what innovation pupils experience as participants in the spaces created by the school.

4. The fourth and final phase of the model concerns entrepreneurship – initiating something one believes in and wants to realize. In this phase it is particularly important that ideas be rooted in the individual, based on a strong identity and an attachment to the place. This helps to ensure ethical choices: that one's actions serve to enhance rather than reduce or destroy the place's qualities. If one is intimately involved with a place, one enters its landscape in the knowledge that it's a common arena requiring cooperation with others, which thereby creates synergies between learning, entrepreneurship and place development. Here, the innovating work of school, teachers and pupils will converge: we write ourselves into the landscape together.

These four fields constitute four stages in a learning and entrepreneurial process that casts schools as leading actors in place development. The model can be used to develop arenas for learning and to develop individual learning processes. We can now fill in the initial sketch to make a complete model, as shown in Figure 15.2. Although the four stages follow a set sequence, there is also a spiral movement in the process. New practice

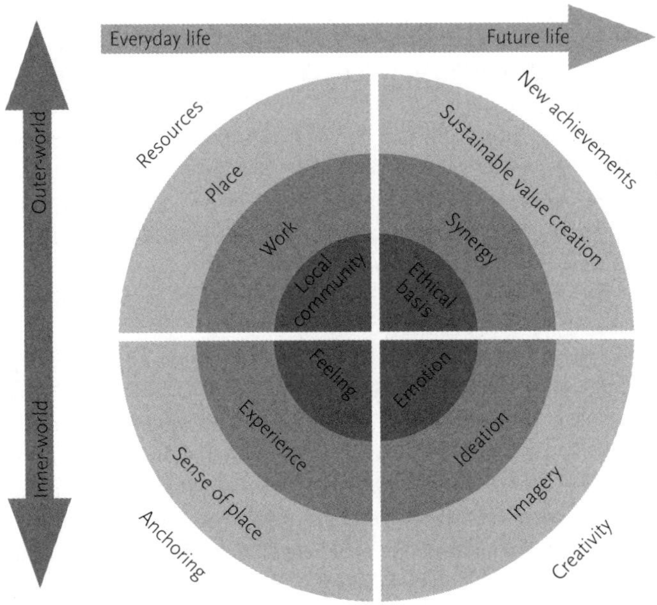

Figure 15.2 Diagram of an innovation process involving school and local community

gradually becomes accepted truth about a place and its resources and potential. And then one must look with new eyes and find new impulses to new innovation. Three keywords are associated with each of the fields within the anchoring, creativity, new praxis. As in Geddes's original diagram, each keyword is also associated with the three others within its circle (inner, middle or outer circle). This brings out what connections are associated with the place and landscape, with the endeavours and work underway and with people's experiences and values.

Inner circle

Here we start with 'folk' as shorthand for a cultural community attached to a place or region. Everyday life is filled with doings, sounds, smells, sights and other things that are familiar to us from an early age. These impressions lodge in the personality and become part of our identification with the place and our roots in it. Gradually, this feeling can meet new impulses arising from travelling to other places, meeting new people, or cultural experiences. These impulses can inspire us to take initiative and strive to do something more, create something new. According to Geddes, when this new action takes effect it will be ethically motivated, being grounded in one's attachment to, and love for, the place. In our case, we can position here both teacher and pupil: the teacher in the process of developing school arenas connected to place, the pupil entering the learning arenas the teacher has provided. Think of schoolchildren picking windfall apples in local gardens and transforming them into a resource, pressing apple juice and selling it to raise funds for their trip abroad in Class 10.

Middle circle[10]

Our point of departure is work and activities – production, theoretical or artistic endeavours, volunteering, clubs and societies, outdoor recreation. All these will provide experiences of actively being in place, as well as a sense of mastering and knowing the place. Remember Patrick, the boy baking flatbread. He lacked initiative and drive, just sat there – until he took a liking to the work. Then something awoke in him that instantly fed into outward action. Or take Ida, the girl who in the end declared an ambition to become a fruit farmer by the fjord. When she met resistance, something happened inside her, igniting a spark: she got a grip on herself and mastered her surroundings in a new way.

Such qualities will be essential in any place-based innovation process. They will help one to envisage how an idea might be formulated and put into practice. Moreover, all processes stand or fall on the quality of cooperation and planning. That's why the middle circle deliberately connects the inner and outer circles. Through a concrete learning task, something is transformed externally in the world, but also internally within the pupil and teacher.

Outer circle

Place is an arena for human activities. It is the foundation of every individual's sense of identity. This, in turn, strongly influences the process of nurturing new creative designs, artistic expression, products and services rooted in the distinctive character of a place.

Education and local curricula in England's national parks

There are ten national parks in England (covering 10 percent of the land area), three in Wales (20 percent) and two in Scotland (7 percent). The youngest English national park is the South Downs, designated in 2011. They are all regarded as vital national assets and play an essential role in forming people's identity. Over half the British population lives within one hour's travel of a national park. These areas are living, working landscapes and may serve as inspiration, not only in the UK but also throughout Europe, for how nature and culture can coevolve and coexist in a sustainable way, within territorial, regional boundaries. The parks recognize not only the outstanding natural qualities of the land but also the intimate and skilful interaction with it in the work of local communities over generations. The learning potential in these social-ecological systems is therefore immense.

The Peak District was one of the first four national parks established in 1951. In 2008, a comprehensive landscape character assessment (LCA) of the variety of natural and cultural landscapes in the park was published. This assessment informed a number of strategies in nature management, local community development and visitor management, as well as in education and voluntary work (Peak District 2009). The LCA is regarded as a very good tool for creating learning spaces within the park.[11]

According to a recent plan for national parks in England, only 10 percent of schoolchildren in England have access to outdoor learning. Yet people in general want children to experience and learn from nature. The government has been supportive of getting more young people out into the national parks: 'We want to engage young people with national parks at every stage of their education' (Department for Environment, Food & Rural Affairs, Environment Agency and Natural England 2016). The first point of its eight-point plan is dedicated to connecting young people with nature.

Although national parks feature in the UK national curriculum, they are treated peripherally and only used as an example. In an attempt to bring national parks into the mainstream, a number of national park authorities have been preparing local curricula. These use the natural assets of the place to facilitate outdoor learning spaces: teaching maths or renewable energy in a stream, for example, or history through a cultural landscape.

A school well along in its efforts is Dulverton Middle School, in Exmoor National Park, which has fully defined itself as an entrepreneurial actor in the local community. It presents its curriculum as follows:

> The Exmoor Curriculum is a unique learning opportunity provided by this school. It is designed to encourage children to engage in learning about and within their home area, giving them a sense of place and belonging. It is a four-year Programme developed with the assistance of the Exmoor National Park Authority and the Exmoor Society. Children work on the four year course to eventually become Junior Exmoor Rangers.[12]

South Downs National Park has chosen a different approach. The national park's educational team offer outdoor learning programmes to visiting classes, helping them to fulfil requirements of the national curriculum (Department of Education 2014). They have developed a resources toolbox for local schools within the national park. They offer consultation and advisory support to teachers in how to adapt learning goals in each of the four Key Stages to their local environment in such a way as to 'bring learning alive and engage the learners'.[13]

Some concluding words about educational ecopreneurship

How can schools develop local place-based curricula? The Aurland model was our starting point. By demonstrating how to identify local resources, and with examples of projects developed through local and regional cooperation, we wish to provide inspiration and methodological anchoring points that will enable you to develop place-based curricula for your school and community. Reversed curriculum planning is a simple tool that enables schools and teachers to develop local curricula and remain able to show parents and authorities how they are covering subjects' learning outcomes – how the educational outcome is not less but more valuable than if the same process were confined to a classroom.

How can schools develop their role as actors in local development? To a great extent the answer is that drawing up and exploring local curricula is place development. The shaping of place-based curricula is comparable to innovation processes in culture and business. It requires an open and searching attitude to how an inner idea and vision may be realized in the outside world. The vision must build on a value base that is made explicit and can be shared by a wider community. The key is to link aims and processes of education and the learner's inner development to processes of the outer development of the place they belong to. This double aim, to grow people *and* place, is the hallmark of educational ecopreneurship.

Ecopreneurship is therefore just as important for the teachers as for the students. The aim is to take leadership to make a difference towards a sustainable future, based on our own values, local resources and trends in society. It is not just a question of learning outcomes. It is about joy and love of creativity and being on a journey that reconnects us to the forces of life and gives us a sense of responsibility.

NOTES

1. Today the Norwegian University of Life Sciences (NMBU).
2. www.abu.skule.no, 'Levande skule, ein lokal plan i entreprenørskap for 2013/14'.
3. The 'huldrefolk' (also 'hulders') or 'hidden people' are reputed to live underground or inside mountains.
4. The 'Sogne boat' is a traditional clinker-built open boat with four oars.
5. http://ninachildrenhome.org/
6. The huldrefolk have parallels in the folklore of many countries. It was said that a piece of steel thrown over their head would bind them to you.
7. Tanzanian goats are not bred for milk production. Crossbreeding produces a stock that is robust and has the milking capacity of Norwegian goats.
8. http://mgetasfriends.com
9. http://www.ameliaearhart.com/about/quotes.html
10. Geddes's formulation.
11. Statement from focus group meeting with planning, management and education officers in Peak District National Park administration, 11 April 2016, Aldern House, Bakewell.
12. http://www.dulvertonmiddleschool.co.uk/curriculum.asp
13. http://learning.southdowns.gov.uk/learning/curriculum

GLOSSARY

Action research is a reflective process of progressive problem-solving, either by individuals working in teams or as part of a community of practice, to improve the way that issues are addressed and problems solved.

Competence-building refers collectively to the nurturing of skills and capacities.

Cultural landscape is a term applied to rural areas with a mosaic of cultivated land, farmsteads, roads and vegetation structures like field verges and allées, connoting its historical significance.

Enactment analysis is a phenomenological approach to reveal all aspects of 'will at work' in engagement with a given task or material within a spatial and social context, in order to unveil what skills, capacities and virtues may be nurtured.

Infields are cultivated land, notably arable land, hayfields and pastures close to (often surrounding) the farmyard. These fields are commonly enclosed by wooden fences.

Local place-based curriculum design is a method to shape a structure of learning spaces and a sequence of learning paths based on engagement, discovery, activities and experiences in real-life spaces outside the classroom.

Outfields consist mainly of semi-cultivated hayfields and natural meadows and pastures. In past times coppiced tree groves occupied a significant part of the outfields.

Reversed curriculum planning is a method by which place-based curriculum design is linked and translated back to relevant national curriculum frameworks to show how it fulfils them.

Situated learning analysis is a reflective method to reveal the pedagogical value of engagement with a particular activity or material in a particular space for a particular student or student group.

Tun is the heart of a Norwegian farm and encompasses the central farm buildings, the open yard and attached gardens.

BIBLIOGRAPHY

Albæk, M. (2013) 'Psykologiske traumer og hjernens utvikling'. https://www.youtube.com/watch?v=yJc9IOGOfgY

Antonovsky, A. (1987) *Unraveling the Mystery of Health: How People Manage Stress and Stay Well.* San Francisco: Jossey-Bass.

Arendt. H. (1977) *Between Past and Future: Exercises in Political Thought.* New York: Penguin.

Asbjørnsen, P.C. and Moe, J. (2017). *Norwegian Folk Tales*, trans. P. Shaw. Oslo: Font Forlag.

Barane, J. (2007) 'Å bli til: Staden, dialogen og forteljinga'. Master's thesis, Rudolf Steinerhøyskolen.

Biesta, G. (2006) *Beyond Learning: Democratic Education for a Human Future.* Boulder, CO: Paradigm.

Biesta, G. (2013) *The Beautiful Risk of Education.* Boulder, CO: Paradigm.

Billington, J. (2010) *Respectfully Quoted: A Dictionary of Quotations.* Washington, D. C.: Library of Congress.

Birgisson, B. (2013) *Den svarte vikingen.* Oslo: Spartakus forlag.

Bly, R. and Hedin, R. (2008) *The Dream We Carry: Selected and Last Poems of Olav H. Hauge.* Port Townsend, WA: Copper Canyon Press.

Boardman, P. (1978) *The Worlds of Patrick Geddes: Biologist, Town Planner, Re-educator, Peace Warrior.* London: Routledge & Kegan Paul.

Dahlin, B. (2004) *Om undran innför livet: Barn och livsfrågor i ett mangkulturelt samhälle.* Lund: Studentlitteratur.

Dahlin, B. (2010) 'The Aporia of Education: An Essay on Derrida's Aporetic Ethics and Nietzsche's Intellectual Conscience'. *Nordic Studies in Eduation*, 30: 166–179.

Dahlin, B., Dösbo, R.I. and Dahlin, K. (2002) *Besjelat lärande: Skisser til en fordjupat pedagogik.* Lund: Studentlitteratur.

Danbolt, G., Loge, Ø. and Wexelsen, E. (2005) *Nikolai Astrup: Tilhørighet og identitet.* Oslo: Labyrinth Press.

Defries, A. (1927) *The Interpreter Geddes: The Man and His Gospel.* London: Routledge & Kegan Paul.

Department for Education (2014) 'National Curriculum'. https://www.gov.uk/government/collections/national-curriculum

Department for Environment, Food & Rural Affairs, Environment Agency and Natural England (2016) 'National Parks: 8-Point Plan for England (2016 to 2020)'. https://www.gov.uk/government/publications/national-parks-8-point-plan-for-england-2016-to-2020

Dewey, J. (2005) *Art as Experience.* New York: Peregee Books.

Dreyfus, H.L. and Dreyfus, S.E. (1986) *Mind over Machine: The Power of Human Intuition and Expertise in the Era of the Computer.* New York: Free Press.

Eriksson, M. and Lindström, B. (2006) 'Antonovsky's Sense of Coherence Scale and the Relation with Health: A Systematic Review'. *Journal of Epidemiology and Community Health*, 60(5): 376–381.

Flor, H. (1982) *Johannes Vinjum*. Oslo: Collage Press.

Førde, A., Kramvig, B., Dale, B., Engan, B. and Gunnerud, N. (2013) *Å finne sted: Metodologiske perspektiver i stedsanalyser*. Trondheim: Akademika forlag.

Gersie, A., Nanson, A. and Schieffelin, E. (eds) (2014) *Storytelling for a Greener World: Environment, Community and Storybased Learning*. Stroud: Hawthorn Press.

Goethe, J.W. von (1970) *Italian Journey*, trans. W.H. Auden and Elizabeth Mayer. Harmondsworth: Penguin Books.

Greve, A. (2005) 'Synet for stedet'. In: Wexelsen, E. (ed.), *Nikolai Astrup: Tilhørighet og identitet*. Oslo: Labyrinth Press.

Hauge, O.H. (1961) *På ørnetuva*. Oslo: Noregs boklag.

Haugsbø, T.K. (2011) 'Fortida gjennom notida'. Ph.D. thesis, University of Bergen. http://nikolai-astrup.no/

Haukeland, P.I. (2008) *Dyp glede: Med Arne Næss inn i dypøkologien*. Oslo: Flux.

Havel V. (2004) *Om håpet*. Oslo: Tidsskriftet Kristensamfunnet.

Hegge, H. (1989) *Frihet, individualitet og samfunn*. Oslo: Universitetsforlaget.

Hegge, H. (1993) 'Mennesket og naturen: naturforståelsen gjennom tidene, med særlig henblikk på vår tids miljøkrise'. In: Hofseth, P. and Vinje, A. (eds), *Økologi, økofilosofi*, pp. 117–141. Oslo: Gyldendal.

Hiim, H. and Hippe, E. (2001) *Å utdanne profesjonelle yrkesutøvere: Yrkesdidaktikk og yrkeskunnskap*. Oslo: Gyldendal.

Holdrege, C. (2014) *Thinking Like a Plant: A Living Science for Life*. New York: Lindisfarne Books.

Hugo, A. (1995) 'Erkjennelsens berøring med livet'. D.Sc. thesis, Norges landbrukshøyskole.

Hugo A. (2002) 'Når faget vokser ut av fenomenene. Naturen som historieforteller'. Seksjon for læring og lærerutdanning, Norges landbrukshøyskole. http://litteratursll.umb-sll.wikispaces.net/file/view/ARTIKKEL+Når+faget+vokser- +ut+av+fenomenene.pdf

Hüter, G. (2004) *The Compassionate Brain: How Empathy Creates Intelligence*. Göttingen: Vandenhoeck & Ruprecht.

Illeris, K. (2013) *Transformativ læring og identitet*. Copenhagen: Samfundslitteratur.

Ingold T. (2000) *The Perception of the Environment. Essays on Livelihood, Dwelling and Skill*. London: Routledge.

Jakobsen, T.G. (2005) *Økofilosofi – økologi, evolusjonsteori og transformativ læring*. Trondheim: Tapir Akademisk Forlag.

Jørgensen, M. W. and Phillips, L. (1999) *Diskursanalyse som teori og metode*. Roskilde: Roskilde Universitetsforlag.

Kommunal- og moderniseringsdepartementet (2015) 'Den europeiske landskapskonvensjonen'. https://www.regjeringen.no/nb/tema/plan-bygg-og- eiendom/plan--og-bygningsloven/plan/internasjonalt-plansamarbeid/landskaps- konvensjonen/id410080/

Krogh, E. (2010) 'School Farm Cooperation in Norway: Background and Recent Research'. www.livinglearning.org

Kunnskapsdepartementet (2012) 'Kunnskap for en felles framtid. Revidert strategi for utdanning for bærekraftig utvikling (2012–2015)'. https://www.regjeringen.no/globalassets/upload/kd/vedlegg/uh/rapporter_og_planer/strategi_ for_ubu.pdf

Kvaløy Setreng, S. (2014) *Elvetid*. Nord-Torpa: Naturveiviser.

Lave, J. and Wenger, E. (1991) *Situated Learning: Legitimate Peripheral Participation*. Cambridge: Cambridge University Press.

Lindgren, L. (2014) 'Praktisk kunnskap under press'. http://www.forskerforum.no/wip4/praktisk-kunnskap-under-press/d.epl?id=2189301

Lindø, R. (1988) *Eventyrskolen*. Oslo: Cappelen.

Ljøsne A.G. (1993) *Naturen og menneskeverket: Vår gamle trearkitektur i nytt lys*. Oslo: Solum Forlag.

Loge, Ø. (2005) 'Hvorfor Nikolai Astrup i 2005?' In: Wexelsen, E., Danbolt, G. and Loge, Ø. (eds), *Nikolai Astrup. Tilhørighet og Identitet*, pp. 176–198. Oslo: Labyrinth Press.

Lorange, E. (1977) *Regional tenkning: Betingelse for god planlegging*. Oslo: Universitetsforlaget.

Massey, D. (1997) 'En global stedsfølelse'. In: Aspen, J. and Pløger, J. (eds), *På sporet av byen. Lesninger av senmoderne byliv*, pp. 306–318. Oslo: Spartacus forlag.

Matthews, P. (2007) *Words in Place. Reconnecting with Nature through Creative Writing*. Stroud: Hawthorn Press.

Molander, B. (1993) *Kunnskap i handling*. Gothenburg: Daidalos.

NCC (1997) 'Core Curriculum for Primary, Secondary and Adult Education in Norway', Royal Ministry of Education, Research and Church Affairs. https://www.udir.no/upload/larerplaner/generell_del/Core_Curriculum_English.pdf

Norberg-Schulz, C. (1993) *Nattlandene: Om byggekunst i Norden*. Oslo: Gyldendal.

Nordahl, T. (2007) *Hjem og skole. Hvordan skape et bedre samarbeid*. Oslo: Universitetsforlaget.

Nordal, S. (2006) *Fysikkens levende sammenhenger: Praksisteorier i kontekstualisert fysikkundervisning*. Ås: Universitetet for miljø- og biovitenskap.

Nyhus, K.A. (2009) *U Alminnelig – Jon Fosse og mystikken*. Follese: Efrem forlag.

Ohnstad, A. (1991) *Glimt frå Aurlandssoga: Samling av artiklar frå Aurland, skriftstyrar Anders Ohnstad*. Aurland: Aurland Sogelag.

Østergaard, E. (2004) 'Hemmelige rom. Komponeringens slektskap med mysteriet'. In: Guldbrandsen, E.E. and Varkøy, Ø. (eds), *Musikk og mysterium: Fjorten essay om grensesprengende musikalsk erfaring*, pp. 91–110. Oslo: Cappelen Damm Akademisk.

Palmer, P.J. (1990) *The Active Life: A Spirituality of Work, Creativity, and Caring*. San Francisco: Harper & Row.

Parow, K. (2000) *Det store spelet: Garden som pedagogisk ressurs*. Oslo: Det Norske Hageselskap.

Phillips, A. (2005) 'Landscape as a Meeting Ground'. In: Brown, J., Mitchell, N. and Beresford M. (eds), *The Protected Landscape Approach: Linking Nature, Culture and Community*. https://portals.iucn.org/library/efiles/ documents/2005-006.pdf

Plieninger, T. and Bieling, C. (2012) 'Connecting Cultural Landscapes to Resilience'. In: Plieninger, T. and Bieling, C. (eds), *Resilience and the Cultural Landscape*, pp. 3–26. Cambridge: Cambridge University Press.

Schön, D. (1984) *Educating the Reflective Practitioner. How Professionals Think in Action*. New York: Perseus Books.

Selman, P. (2012) *Sustainable Landscape Planning. The Reconnection Agenda*. London: Routledge.

Setreng, S.K. (2014) 'Om oss', *Naturveiviser*. http://www.naturveiviser.no/?page_id=17

Sigman, A. (2010) 'Practically Minded:. The Benefits and Mechanism Associated with Craft Based Curriculum'. http://rmt.org/pdf/Brantwood/brantwood-practically-minded---research-into-a-practical-curriculum%20-%20Copy.pdf

Spitzer, M. (1999) *The Mind within the Net: Models of Learning, Thinking and Acting*. Cambridge, MA: MIT Press.

Spurkeland, J. (2011) *Relasjonspedagogikk. Samhandling og resultater i skolen*. Bergen: Fagbokforlaget.

Stokland, O. (1969) *Av Norges indre historie*. Oslo: Dreyer.

Sturluson, S. (2005) *The Prose Edda: North Mythology*, trans. J.L. Byock. London: Penguin.

Sundland, E. (1995) *Det var en gang et menneske. Tolkninger av Asbjørnsen og Moes undereventyr som allegorier på menneskelig innsikt og erkjennelse*. Oslo: Cappelen Akademisk.

Surti, B.S. (1981) *Thus Spoke Zarathustra*. Chennai: Sri Ramakrishna Math.

Svarstad, M. (2012) *Da sannheten fikk klærne på. En innføring i muntlig fortellerkunst*. Oslo: Biblioteksentralen.

Taylor, E.W. (2008) *Transformative Learning Theory*. Hoboken, NJ: John Wiley.

Tilbury, D., Stevenson, R.B., Fien, J. and Schreuder, D. (2002) *Education and Sustainability: Responding to the Global Challenge*. Gland: Commission on Education and Communication, International Union for Conservation and Nature.

Utdanningsdirektoratet (2006) 'Læreplanverket for Kunnskapsløftet i grunnskolen og i videregående opplæring danner fundamentet for opplæringen i skole og bedrift'. http://www.udir.no/Lareplaner/Kunnskapsloftet/

Utdanningsdirektoratet (2012) 'Kunnskap for en felles framtid. Revidert strategi for utdanning for bærekraftig utvikling (2012–2015)'. https://www.regjeringen.no/globalassets/upload/kd/vedlegg/uh/rapporter_og_planer/strategi_ for_ubu.pdf

Vinjum, E. (2009) *Johannes Vinjum: Bror og biletkunstnar*. Hokksund: Erlend Vinjum.

Welter, V. (2002) *Biopolis*. Cambridge, MA: MIT Press.

Wright, D., Camden-Pratt, C. and Hill, S. (eds) (2011) *Social Ecology: Applying Ecological Understanding to Our Lives and Our Planet*. Stroud: Hawthorn Press.

ABOUT THE AUTHORS

Jorunn Barane, born in 1961, grew up on an island on the west coast of Norway. She lives with her family in Aurland, a small village in Sognefjord, surrounded by high mountains and waterfalls. She lectures at Sogn Agriculture College (www.sjh.no) in Ecopreneurship, drama and storytelling (www.naturpedagog.no) She trained as a Waldorf teacher, and has a Masters in environmental education.

Jorunn has been researching and teaching ecology, pedagogy and storytelling from kindergarten to high school for 25 years. She helps people to find their potential and values in dialogue with the living earth. Her research question is: How can we take the lead in building living communities for a sustainable future? The world is evolving, and it is a continuing creative process to develop our senses of belonging and identity with place and community. And we have to use all our courage and imagination to look at what's not yet there, building space for the future. We can exercise the ability to find and tell traditional stories and myths of ecology and hope, find the willpower and search for spiritual helpers like the Ashlad did. This work encourages also craft-based and artistic ways of working. Jorunn runs courses in place-based learning and entrepreneurship for teachers, students, farmers and communities.

Aksel Hugo, born 1959, studied biology, agroecology, and natural resource management at the Norwegian University of Life Sciences (NULS). These studies led to a deep interest in 'the nature of knowing nature' and a PhD in philosophy of education. He developed an interest in enactment analysis – studying the nature of different ways of knowing, in particular how the spiritual activity of attention moves, dialogues and connects thinking with the realm of the senses, and the cognitive realm with embodied ways of knowing. These studies led to an interest in the epistemology and pedagogy of Rudolf Steiner and Waldorf Education, and many years of practice as a science teacher in a local Waldorf School.

For years he combined being a practitioner with being a researcher and teacher-educator in phenomenological science education at NULS. From 2005–2012 he directed a state-approved master programme in Waldorf Education delivered at the Rudolf Steiner University College in Oslo. From this international MA, a close collaboration with Ruskin Mill Trust and their Research Centre was developed, leading to three years collaborative action research, as the research coordinator of the RMT Field Centre, from 2013-2016.

Morten Clemetsen, born 1956, decided to study landscape architecture after discovering farmers' creative impact on the rural environment when working as an agricultural assistant in a west Norwegian farming community. After completing a PhD on the landscape dimension in sustainable agriculture, he moved back to West Norway. He founded of Aurland Nature Works, a consultancy for landscape and asset based community development. He has a long time experience in participatory community development processes based on tangible and intangible landscape and cultural heritage resources. He has also a long record in facilitating voluntary working groups in cultural landscape management and restoration of rural vernacular buildings in the West Norwegian fjord landscapes. Currently he is Professor in rural landscape and community planning at the Norwegian University of Life Sciences.

INDEX

Other Books from Hawthorn Press

Social Ecology

Applying ecological understanding to our lives and our planet

Edited by David Wright, Catherine Camden-Pratt, Stuart Hill

Social Ecology addresses the burning question of how to apply ecological understanding to every aspect of our lives. The 27 contributors share their experiences in this 'coming of age' anthology of keynote articles. The book provides a holistic framework for change, based on the interrelationships between the personal, social, environmental and 'spiritual', helping us understand how we got here, and how to realise more sustainable, caring futures.

336pp; 234 × 156mm; pb; 978-1-907359-11-8

The Natural Storyteller

Wildlife Tales for Telling

Georgiana Keable

Here is a handbook full of fairytales from the forest and true tales of sea, earth and sky. With story maps, brain-teasing riddles, story skeletons and adventures, here is a vibrant invitation to embrace a world of stories all about nature, animals and plants – and our relationship with them. This diverse collection will nurture active literacy skills, helping children to form an essential bond with nature.

272pp; 228 x 186mm; pb; 9781907359804

ORDERING BOOKS

If you have difficulties ordering Hawthorn Press books from a bookshop, you can order direct from our website **www.hawthornpress.com**, or from our UK distributor BookSource, 50 Cambuslang Road, Glasgow, G32 8NB Tel: (0845) 370 0063 Email: orders@booksource.net.

Hawthorn Press

A full list of our non-UK distributors can be found on our website.